MW01196961

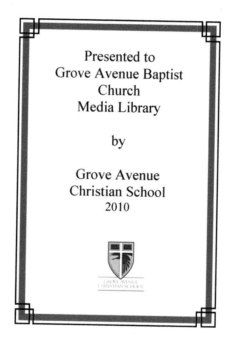

Decades of American History

AMERICA IN THE 1900s AND 1910s

JIM CALLAN

Facts On File, Inc.

To Stella, who's given me my favorite decade

A Stonesong Press Book
Decades of American History: *America in the 1900s and 1910s*

Facts On File, Inc.
132 West 31st Street
New York NY 10001

Library of Congress Cataloging-in-Publication Data

Callan, Jim.
   America in the 1900s and 1910s / Jim Callan.
          p. cm. — (Decades of American history)
   "A Stonesong Press book."
   Includes bibliographical references and index.
   Audience: Grades 4–9.
   ISBN 0-8160-5636-6
1.   United States—History—1901–1909—Juvenile literature. 2.   United
States—History—1909–1913—Juvenile literature. 3.   United
States—History—1913–1921—Juvenile literature. 4.   Nineteen hundreds
(Decade)—Juvenile literature. 5.   Nineteen tens—Juvenile literature.
I. Title. II. Series.
   E756.C35 2005
   973.91'1—dc22
                                                                      2004018946

Facts On File books are available at special discounts when purchased in bulk quantities
for businesses, associations, institutions, or sales promotions. Please call our Special Sales
Department in New York at (212) 967-8800 or (800) 322-8755.

The Stonesong Press and Facts On File, Inc. wish to thank the Crisis Publishing Co., Inc.,
the publisher of the magazine of the National Association for the Advancement of
Colored People, for the use of the illustration reproduced on p. 80.

You can find Facts On File on the World Wide Web at http://www.factsonfile.com

Text design by Laura Smyth, Smythetype
Photo research by Larry Schwartz
Cover design by Pehrsson Design

Printed in the United States of America

VB PKG 10 9 8 7 6 5 4

This book is printed on acid-free paper.

CONTENTS

CHAPTER 1

A NEW CENTURY BEGINS, AMERICA IN 1900

AS THE YEAR 1900 APPROACHED, MOST Americans faced the new 20th century with a feeling of tremendous confidence. They had many reasons to feel hopeful about the future. The economy was strong, and the country was at peace. Thirty-five years earlier, the United States had survived its greatest test—the Civil War (1861–65). The recent U.S. victory in the Spanish-American War (1898) had turned the nation into a world power with a strong military. The western frontier had been settled, and the growing railroad system was both expanding the country's horizons and bringing the American people closer together.

At the turn of the century, most Americans still lived on farms like this one in Iowa. *(Library of Congress)*

The first decade of the 20th century has been called the Age of Innocence, the Age of Optimism, and the Age of Confidence. At the turn of the century, Americans expected nothing but peace, prosperity, and progress, and for the first decade—the 1900s—they would get it. To understand this decade, however, one must look at a few key events of the late 19th century that shaped the new era and set the stage for the 20th century.

THE SPANISH-AMERICAN WAR AND COLONIAL EXPANSION

In January 1898, President William McKinley sent the battleship USS *Maine* to the Spanish colony of Cuba to protect American interests. The major U.S. interest in the island was sugar. American companies had invested $50 million in Cuba, and its sugar trade was one of America's most profitable businesses. The United States had tried to purchase Cuba from Spain for many years, but the colony had equal trade importance for Spain. Puerto Rico and Cuba were the last remnants in the Western Hemisphere of Spain's once-extensive empire.

The Cubans had been fighting for independence from Spain since 1868. In 1896, Spain declared martial

With help from the yellow journalists of the era, the explosion of the *Maine* triggered the Spanish-American War. This image is from the *New York World,* February 17, 1898. *(Library of Congress)*

THE WORLD'S PHOTOGRAPH OF THE MAINE WRECK.

This photograph (the first published) was taken by the World's Staff Correspondent at Havana on Wednesday morning, after the night explosion; the photograph left Havana by steamship Olivette at 2 P. M. Wednesday, arrived at Key West at 10.30 P. M.; at Port Tampa, Fla., 4 P. M. Thursday; left Tampa by New York express at 7 P. M. Thursday, and arrived at New York at 2.15 yesterday afternoon. It is here reproduced exactly. The original photograph was shown to Admiral Erben and other naval experts by World reporters last night.

law in the colony and moved the civilian population into a central area guarded by Spanish troops. Americans were outraged by this, and the press fueled the anti-Spanish feeling in the country. Newspapers at the time used a sensational approach to reporting, called yellow journalism, to sell papers. (Yellow journalism got its name from The Yellow Kid, a popular cartoon character in William Randolph Hearst's *New York Journal* at the turn of the century.) The *New York Journal* was one of the leaders of yellow journalism, and it was often accused of creating the news rather than reporting it. Hearst once cabled his photographer in Cuba, saying "You furnish the pictures, I'll furnish the war."

On February 15, 1898, the *Maine* exploded and sank in Havana harbor. There was never any evidence that the Spanish were responsible, but the American public believed otherwise. The United States declared war on Spain on April 25, 1898. The war was fought on two fronts, in Cuba and the Philippines, a Spanish colony in the Pacific Ocean. In the Philippines, U.S. commodore George Dewey quickly destroyed the Spanish fleet in Manila Bay. In Cuba, victory was just as swift, and within three months Spain surrendered. At the battle of San Juan Hill, future U.S. president Teddy Roosevelt led a decisive charge that helped win the war and made him an American hero.

The war officially ended with the signing of the Treaty of Paris on December 10, 1898. It was an important turning point in U.S. history. As a result of the treaty, the United States acquired Cuba, the Philippines, Puerto Rico, and the Pacific island of Guam. After a long debate in Congress, President McKinley decided to keep all these islands as colonies rather than grant them independence.

Within just two years, U.S. colonial holdings grew even more extensive. In 1898, the United States also annexed the previously independent Hawaiian Islands in the Pacific, again primarily to protect a profitable

Immigrants from Europe arrived on the East Coast after sometimes rough Atlantic Ocean crossings. *(Library of Congress)*

sugarcane business owned by Americans. In 1899, half of the Samoan Islands, also in the Pacific, became another U.S. colony. The United States was changing into a world colonial power.

IMMIGRATION

The United States has always been a nation of immigrants, but starting in the 1880s, the numbers began soaring. From 1880 to 1890, 5.3 million immigrants came to the United States, and from 1890 to 1900, another 3.7 million left their homelands for U.S. shores. By 1900, America's population was about 76 million, double what it had been just 30 years earlier, and almost one-third of the population were either immigrants or children of immigrants. Some came seeking liberty from oppressive governments, while others came to seek economic opportunity. They wanted a better life financially in the United States, where they had heard "the streets were paved with gold," as a popular saying held.

During the first great wave of immigration, the three decades between 1850 and 1880, about 7.7 million

THE BOXER REBELLION

America's victory in the Spanish-American War in 1898 made it a world power. It would not take long for that power to be tested. During the 1890s, a movement started in China opposing all foreign influence in that nation. The movement was started by a group called the Righteous and Harmonious Fists. They were also known as the Boxers because they practiced gymnastics and other exercises. The Boxers had strong support in China including from the ruling government.

In 1900, the Boxers started to destroy everything that they considered foreign. They burned foreign churches, schools, and homes. They killed missionaries, Chinese Christians, and anyone who supported foreign ideas. The Boxers then forced all foreign diplomats to take refuge in the British Embassy in Peking (now

Beijing) and laid siege to the embassy. Officials inside the embassy included diplomats from England, Russia, Germany, and France as well as Americans. When the diplomats called for military help from their home countries, the Chinese government declared war on each one of them.

President McKinley sent 5,000 troops to join forces from eight other nations. The forces put down the rebellion and lifted the siege against the embassy. In the peace settlement, China agreed to execute several Boxer officials, destroy many forts, and pay more than $300 million in damages. The United States also used the settlement to extend its open-door trade policy with China. The open door policy sought to give all countries equal access to the profitable trade in China.

immigrants had come to the United States. For the most part, these immigrants had little trouble adapting to American life. They came from England, Ireland, Germany, and Scandinavia and settled on farms in rural America. The United States was still an agricultural society in the 19th century. Farming offered a familiar way for these immigrants to make a living, and they were encouraged to move to the less populated frontier areas by the U.S. government with land grants and sales. These immigrants also were accepted fairly easily because their customs, their primarily Protestant religion, and often their languages were similar to those of Americans. Among these groups, the Irish had the most difficulty being accepted. They faced more prejudice because of their Catholic religion and their tendency to remain in urban areas.

On the Pacific coast, immigration from China increased significantly in the mid-19th century. The main reasons for this increase were the many jobs available building the western railroads and the discovery of gold in California in 1848. These Chinese

By 1900, one-third of America's population were immigrants. Most lived in overcrowded urban areas. *(Library of Congress)*

A *Kansas City Journal* cartoon shows prejudice against immigrants. *(National Park Service—Ellis Island Immigration Museum)*

Chinese immigrants, like this young boy, mainly came to the West Coast.
(*Library of Congress*)

"You press the button and we do the rest."

—Kodak slogan for its new $1 Brownie Box Camera

immigrants faced harsh working and living conditions and unfamiliar customs and language. During the late 1870s, Californians demanded laws limiting Chinese immigration. Angry mobs even attacked Chinese immigrants, who were accused of lowering wages, creating unfair business competition, and taking jobs away from Americans. In 1882, Congress passed a law suspending Chinese immigration for 10 years.

The face of immigration began to change dramatically in the 1890s. Political and economic unrest in Europe drove new immigrants from Southern and Eastern Europe to American shores. Most immigrants to the United States in this decade were Italians, Slavs, and Jews with very different customs, religions, and languages. Most of rural America had been settled, and farmland was less available. Most of the new immigrants headed for the big cities in the Northeast where factory jobs were available. New York, Chicago, and Philadelphia saw huge increases in their populations in the final decades of the 19th century. The United States was becoming an urban society.

THE INDUSTRIAL REVOLUTION

The simplest definition of the Industrial Revolution is the widespread replacement of manual labor by machines. The Industrial Revolution began in Great Britain in the 18th century with three main discoveries. First, British scientists and engineers found a way to use coal to produce iron from iron ore. The iron was put to many uses, including the building of Britain's railroads, which greatly improved transportation and made commerce much easier. The second discovery involved the improvement of the steam engine. The steam engine was originally used only in mining to pump water from the underground mines. Improvements to the steam engine in the mid–18th century allowed steam engines to be used for power in many different industries. The third discovery came in the textile, or cloth-making, business. With the invention of weaving and spinning machines, cloth could now be produced at tremendous speed and in great quantities.

The beginnings of the Industrial Revolution in the United States came in the late 18th century when American industries started using English inventions. One of the first was the spinning jenny, invented by England's James Hargreaves around 1764. The machine increased textile production by allowing workers to spin many different cotton threads at once. The industry grew until large textile mills were producing huge amounts of clothing, which could be bought at a market rather than made at home.

Another important step in the industrialization of the American economy was the use of interchangeable parts and the assembly line. In 1798, Eli Whitney

"I owe the public nothing."

—J. P. Morgan when asked to justify the difference in his wealth and the general public

As America became industrialized, many women found work in the new factories and plants opening in the big cities. *(Library of Congress)*

A Gibson Girl–type suffragist lends her enthusiasm to the cause. *(Library of Congress)*

THE IDEAL WOMAN AT THE TURN OF THE CENTURY

The turn of the century brought the first so-called ideal woman for American women to copy. It was the Gibson Girl. Charles Dana Gibson was an artist for *Life* magazine when he first started drawing his ideal. She quickly became the model for an entire generation of American women.

In Gibson's drawings, the Gibson Girl was tall, with hair piled up in a thick pompadour on top of her head. She was poised, stylishly dressed and, most of all, extremely pretty. "At last, the typical American girl," wrote one reporter.

Gibson Girls started appearing everywhere—on dinner plates, pillowcases, magazine ads, even wallpaper. The most famous living example of a Gibson Girl was Teddy Roosevelt's daughter, Alice. Alice was so idolized by American women that many named their babies after her and wore her favorite color, Alice blue. There was even a song written in her honor, "Alice, Where Art Thou." Alice Roosevelt's wedding in 1905 was the social event of the decade.

signed a contract with the federal government to produce 10,000 military muskets. He built a factory near New Haven, Connecticut, where he created a factory system of producing the parts of the muskets on an assembly line of workers. The system consistently allowed for the production of the same products. The factory system would slowly replace individual craftsmen as the primary method of manufacturing.

By the mid– to late 19th century, the United States had became the leader of the Industrial Revolution. There were two main reasons for this. First, the United States was a vast land with huge amounts of raw materials such as coal and wood. By 1900, the United States was producing one-third of the world's coal, steel, and iron. Second, by the final decades of the 19th century, immigration was making America's population soar by more than 1 million per year. America's booming population created a large work force for the new industries that were developing and a huge market for new products.

The vast size of the country presented challenges that encouraged American inventors to take the lead in two areas of technology: communication and transportation. The telegraph was invented by American Samuel Morse in 1844. This allowed messages to be sent instantly over long distances using electronic codes and cable wire. By 1866, international cable had been laid, connecting nearly the entire world by telegraph. In 1876, American Alexander Graham Bell invented the telephone. Americans also started building a huge railroad system. By 1860, the United States had more than half the railroad tracks in the world, and the first transcontinental railroad was completed in 1869. The United States was becoming an industrial society.

> **By 1900, the United States had 198,000 miles of railroad track across the country.**

WORKERS AND WORKING CONDITIONS

By 1900, many Americans faced great changes in how they lived and worked. They had many reasons for optimism, but there were serious new problems, too. As manufacturing became the driving force of the U.S. economy, hundreds of factories and plants opened in the big cities. America's rail lines and ports bustled with the transport of goods. This economic boom required huge numbers of workers, and the United States had a ready work force in its immigrant population. As technology slowly began to reduce the need for human labor on farms, many rural workers also headed for jobs in the urban areas.

Members of this new class of industrial worker, however, found terrible working conditions in their new jobs. Because there were so many workers available, business owners offered very low wages and long hours. The workweek was six or even seven days, and the workday was ten to twelve hours long. Job

America's economy was booming in 1900, but many workers, such as these coal miners in Pennsylvania, worked long hours for little pay.
(Library of Congress)

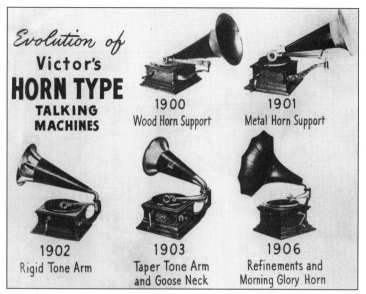

Mass production of goods made entertainment technology such as the phonograph available to many Americans. *(Library of Congress)*

security did not exist. Workers could be fired for any reason, including sickness, and they could be easily replaced.

Working conditions in the factories were usually crowded and unhealthy. The deadly and infectious lung disease of tuberculosis was common and spread easily in the crowded conditions. Coal miners had no protection against black lung disease, which came from inhaling coal dust. No federal laws regulated safety, so precautions were rare in any industry. Even though fire was a common occurrence, most factories had no fire escapes. The United States had the highest accident rate of all industrial nations. Thousands of Americans were killed, crippled, or injured annually while on the job, and no compensation was then available for victims.

CHILD LABOR

One of the most disturbing aspects of the work place at the turn of the century was child labor. In 1900, more than 1 million children, both boys and girls, under the age of thirteen were employed in the country's factories, farms, and mines, some as young as ten years old. Children's pay was often lower than adult pay. Children in coal mines received about fifty cents for a ten-hour workday while adults were paid about ninety cents a day. Injuries were very common, especially in the coal mines and cotton mills, where limbs were easily caught in the machinery. Unfortunately, a family's survival often depended on the extra income a child brought home, so children had no choice but to work as wage earners. This meant many young people were forced into a life of virtual slavery and had no opportunity for an education. Some of the injured were crippled for life, becoming unable earn any kind of a living except as criminals or beggars. Some of the older girls became prostitutes after losing their jobs to younger, lower-paid children.

UNIONS

To try to improve their working conditions, American workers had started to form unions in the 1820s and 1830s. These early unions were called trade unions because they were organized by trades, such as unions of skilled carpenters, masons, and printers. These unions tried to use their power as a group acting together to force employers to raise wages, but business owners made few concessions to the trade unions.

In 1869, the Knights of Labor became the first group to organize workers into a single union rather than into separate trade unions. The Knights of Labor membership was open to anyone except bankers, stock-brokers, lawyers, and liquor manufacturers. In 1885, the union had its first success when a strike forced railroads owned by Jay Gould to meet its demands. The Knights saw its membership rise from 100,000 to 700,000 within a year. The union would quickly lose its influence, however. The following year, the Knights lost a second strike against Gould's railroads and started to decline.

In 1886, the American Federation of Labor (AFL) was formed by 25 trade unions. The AFL was led by Samuel Gompers and consisted of about 140,000 skilled workers. By the end of the century, the AFL had become the strongest force for labor in the country. It helped organize strikes and urged local, state, and federal government to pass laws protecting workers. There were still very few concessions from business leaders however. The trends in labor were very clear. Machinery had lowered the worth of skilled workers and apprentices. The labor of immigrants, women, and children

CONSUMERS AND ADVERTISING

The Industrial Revolution brought about a major change in how Americans bought goods. The mass production of goods made possible by new machinery increased the variety of goods available. For example, clothes used to be made at home. They were now available in many different styles and cheaper than making them at home. All sorts of mechanical gadgets, such as toasters, typewriters, even cars, were also now available to the public. With so many choices, Americans were becoming consumers.

The American market was also increasing with the rise in population and the strong economy. This meant manufacturers had to compete for each consumer's business. Advertising became the most effective way to sell products, especially in the growing number of national magazines. Advertising agencies soon appeared to create memorable ads. They would often use catchphrases to stick in the mind of the consumer, a practice that continues to this day.

By 1900, America was the leader of the Industrial Revolution, producing one-third of the world's coal, steel, and iron. *(Library of Congress)*

In 1895, the U.S. government needed an emergency loan of $65 million. President Grover Cleveland borrowed it from wealthy banker J. P. Morgan.

was replacing the work of skilled tradesmen. This meant lower wages for the workers and huge profits for the business owners, which lead to the growth of a bitter opposition between workers and owners.

BIG BUSINESS

Most Americans believed that hard work could lead to material success. Work was supposed to offer the people a chance at a life in a society marked by equality and fairness. The problem in 1900 was that many thought this "American Dream" was dying. Most of the wealth created by the Industrial Revolution was winding up in very few hands. Just 1 percent of Americans owned half of the country's wealth. Those who controlled the biggest businesses like oil (John D. Rockefeller of Standard Oil), steel (Andrew Carnegie of U.S. Steel) and banking (J. P. Morgan of Northern Securities)

BUILDING SKYWARD

One of the symbols of the future at the turn of the century was the skyscraper. In 1871, a huge fire wiped out downtown Chicago. When engineers and architects started to rebuild the city, they used new and safer building materials such as steel, glass, and concrete. With these stronger materials and the recent invention of the electric elevator, buildings could be made higher. It seemed the United States had conquered the West, so architects now started to conquer the air.

The skyscraper became popular for two main reasons. First, businesses ran more efficiently with offices, warehouses, and banks all in the same building. Second, rising land costs made it cheaper to build upward.

The first skyscraper built was Chicago's Home Insurance Building, completed in 1885. It was 10 stories high. New York City, soon took the lead in having the highest skyscrapers. As they started to rise over New York's skyline, they became an impressive symbol to the immigrants catching their first glimpse of their new homeland. The tallest building in the world in 1900 was New York's Park Row Building. It was 390 feet high with 30 stories.

Skyscrapers began to change the urban skyline at the turn of the century. New York City's Flatiron Building, built in 1902, on Fifth Avenue and 23rd Street, attracted tourists immediately.
(Private Collection)

made fortunes. These businessmen were called robber barons because they used unfair practices to increase their personal profit. For example, they would form what are called trusts, in which one company would acquire other companies so that they could all be run by one man. This would create a monopoly or unfair control over an entire industry.

By 1900, the robber barons had become the most powerful men in the country. No laws existed to control their business practices and acquisition of wealth. Even farming came under their control. Farmers needed the new farming machines and the railroads to transport their products. Much of the American public was angry at these conditions, but government leaders were reluctant to do anything. Government regulation of business or even talks between labor and management were deeply radical ideas at the time. A movement was under way, however, which would attack those issues and many others in American society.

"Give me your tired, your poor, your huddled masses, yearning to breathe free."

—Poet Emma Lazarus's message to America's immigrants later inscribed on the Statue on Liberty

Immigrants often had to live in crowded tenements like this Italian family of seven sharing one room in New York City ca. 1900. *(Library of Congress)*

THE PROGRESSIVE MOVEMENT

The social changes that the United States had undergone in the late 19th century radically altered the nation. Many felt that the most disturbing change was economic. The rich were much richer, and the poor were much poorer. These economic changes dramatically changed American society. As immigrants and rural workers crowded into the big cities, a new lower class evolved. The low wages of their unskilled jobs doomed workers and their families to a life of poverty. The hardships grew even worse as cities found that they could not deal with overpopulation. At the start of the 20th century, it was estimated that half the population of New York City and Chicago lived in poverty.

The quality of life suffered in many ways. Crime increased, and the urban police departments at the time proved inadequate to deal with it. Rising populations stressed city sewer systems, which broke down and

spread filth and disease. Decent housing was rare, in part because there were no building or health codes. Many urban families were forced to live in decaying buildings often sharing a single small room. Their neighborhoods came to be known as slums and their buildings as tenements. To make matters worse, city governments were often corrupt. Officials regularly accepted bribes from business interests to keep money and power in their hands. Few social services were available to the poor.

As the new century began, many Americans believed that the nation needed to change. They felt government should be actively fighting against problems such as poverty, child labor, and business trusts and fighting for workers' rights. Some of these reformers focused on very specific causes such as women's suffrage (right to vote), civil rights for African Americans, and the prohibition of alcohol. This call for reform was called the progressive movement.

Up until 1900, the U.S. government generally practiced an economic theory called laissez-faire. This policy meant that government did not interfere in business or in the economy very much or very often. A large majority of those active in U.S. government believed in personal freedom and individualism so strongly that they seldom supported any government activity to address social change itself. In this view, the government was responsible only for basic services such as military protection, and American politicians were not expected to be social activists. The American people had thrived under this policy for more than a century.

The Progressives rejected that idea. They thought changes in modern America had caused problems so severe that only government action could solve them. They believed both local and federal government had the responsibility to be activist and effect social change, not just provide basic services. They also believed that the federal government was the only force powerful enough to take on big business and the robber barons. Some

Susan B. Anthony was an active leader of the women's suffrage movement from 1853 until her death in 1906, when she passed the torch to a new generation of suffragists. *(Library of Congress)*

Robber barons such as U.S. Steel's Andrew Carnegie controlled most of America's wealth at the turn of the century. *(Library of Congress)*

"In the battle of the slum, we win or we perish. There is no middle ground."

—Jacob Riis in his poverty exposé *How the Other Half Lives*

In 1900, Andrew Carnegie's income was $10 million. The average American yearly income that year was $500.

Progressives, such as the Socialists, adopted radical ideas to deal with the growing problems. They believed that the United States needed an entirely new economic and political system. Another radical idea at the time was anarchism. The anarchists were a small, unorganized group who totally rejected the idea of a larger, more active government and believed that all government was inherently evil and should be destroyed.

The progressive movement started to achieve results first at the local and state level. Some cities passed civil service laws designed to combat corruption. Open tests were given, and jobs went to capable workers rather than the friends and relatives of government officials. Governments started awarding contracts for services such as construction of public buildings through open bidding rather than bribery. The first Progressive governor, Robert La Follette, was elected in 1900 in Wisconsin. He brought about reforms in business regulation, factory safety, income tax, and voting. La Follette would eventually run for president for the Progressive Party in 1924.

MUCKRAKERS

Journalism also changed a great deal over the final decades of the 19th century. New technology made printing cheaper and more efficient. As a result, more pictures and images started to appear in publications. In addition, more Americans were reading newspapers than ever before. In 1870, there were about 600 daily newspapers in the country. By 1899, there were more than 1,600 dailies. In the same time span, daily circulation soared from 3 million to 24 million. As circulation and advertising grew, newspaper editors had many more pages to fill with news. Reporters now needed to find more stories to attract and keep readers.

Some of the new journalism was attacked as yellow journalism, written in an overly exciting or sensational way. Yellow journalism, full of exaggerations and details

THE FOUR HUNDRED

The richest of America's new ultra-rich society were known as the Four Hundred. The phrase was coined by an anonymous socialite after learning that the ballroom of the wealthy Astor family held 400 people. She said that was the right size because there were only 400 people in the country worth inviting to parties.

New York's Fifth Avenue became known as the Gold Coast of the wealthy because it contained many of their luxurious mansions. Families such as the Morgans, Vanderbilts, Goulds, and Astors all owned enormous homes on the Gold Coast, staffed with dozens of servants and stuffed with expensive artworks imported from Europe.

Newport, Rhode Island, became the center of the Four Hundred's summer mansions, but the most ornate of all the mansions was in North Carolina. George Vanderbilt's summer home, the Biltmore Estate, had 250 rooms including 40 bedrooms and more than 200 square miles of land. Its library held more than 250,000 books, and it employed more foresters than the entire U.S. forestry program.

American authors who wrote about this small but fabulously wealthy society include Edith Wharton and Henry James. Many of their novels and stories, such as Wharton's *The House of Mirth* and James's *Washington Square* became popular movies and plays in the later half of the 20th century.

about crime, violence, and prostitution, did attract readers. Some historians claim that yellow journalism sensationalized the Spanish oppression of Cuban independence and actually caused the Spanish-American War.

Not all journalism was yellow, however. Many writers started doing human interest stories. These stories went beyond just informing the reader. They were written in an emotional way to touch the heart of the reader. A common human interest story in a turn of the century newspaper would be concerned with the suffering of the poor in the slums of the big cities. Editors found that these stories not only filled pages but sold newspapers. Papers began to challenge the corruption in government and other institutions that caused this human suffering. These exposés became front page news, and journalists became allies of the Progressive movement. Progressive journalism is generally said to have begun with the book *How the Other Half Lives* by Jacob Riis in 1890. Riis's book exposed the horrible conditions in New York City slums.

Writers who exposed society's problems came to be known as muckrakers. (Teddy Roosevelt coined the term from a character in John Bunyan's 17th-century book,

After serving six years as Wisconsin's governor, Bob La Follette was elected to the U.S. Senate in 1906. *(National Archives)*

A Cahuilla woman looks into the distance in this portrait photograph by Edward Curtis. *(Library of Congress)*

Pilgrim's Progress, whose job was to clear the mud from a barn with a muckrake.) By 1901, muckrakers were writing magazine articles and books exposing America's problems to a larger audience. The first muckraker novel was published that year. Frank Norris's *The Octopus* revealed the American farmers' battle with the strong railroad trust. Many believe that the progressive movement would have had little, if any, success without the muckrakers. The muckraking journalists informed the public of the problems that the Progressives wanted to solve.

AFRICAN AMERICANS AND AMERICAN INDIANS

As horrible as living conditions were for many in America's urban slums, two groups had it even worse: African Americans and American Indians. African Americans in the South suffered from both poverty and the brutality of racism. In the Reconstruction years following the Civil War, African Americans had been granted many rights. The Fifteenth Amendment to the Constitution granted them the vital right to vote in 1870.

CARRIE NATION

At the start of the 20th century, there was a strong movement in the United States to ban alcoholic beverages. It was called the temperance movement and supporters blamed alcohol for poverty, health problems, corrupt government, and the destruction of families. Religious leaders in the movement said it led to immoral behavior. One group leading the movement was the Women's Christian Temperance Union, and one of its leaders was Carrie Nation. Most of the women in the group would just hold prayer meetings and give speeches against the evils of drunkenness. Nation had another approach.

Nation had strong religious feelings, and she said she saw visions. She thought that she was protected by God because in 1889 a fire in her town had left her house untouched. She even thought her name was a command from God. Nation decided to try to close the saloons for good. Armed with a hatchet, she entered the saloons and smashed the furniture and bottles of alcohol to pieces.

Nation called her approach "hatchet-ation," and she soon had a small group of followers. She took her hatchet all around the country destroying bars and being arrested. As her fame grew, she also gave speeches at meeting halls and sold souvenir hatchets. Most of the money she made went to her large legal costs. She died in 1911, eight years before an amendment to the Constitution enforced the prohibition of alcohol in 1919. (The amendment would later be repealed in 1933.)

Many southern states, however, found ways to deprive African Americans of their voting rights. States imposed poll taxes and required literacy tests. When poor whites were affected by these restrictions, southern leaders used grandfather clauses in their state constitutions. These clauses gave the right to vote to males whose father or grandfather had voted prior to 1867. This prevented almost all African Americans from voting because prior to 1867 most of their fathers and grandfathers were slaves.

At the start of the 20th century, the lack of voting rights kept African Americans stuck in a cycle of racism and poverty. Many blacks were denied fair trials. Southern justice for African Americans was often a lynching, in which white crowds would hang an African American accused of a crime without a trial. Sometimes the lynchings were treated as entertainment and held in theaters. Antilynching groups began to form.

Some African-American leaders, such as Booker T. Washington, supported education as a way for blacks to end their oppression. Even this idea was radical to many whites. When Booker T. Washington was invited to the White House in 1901, race riots occurred in the South. White racists were so angry that they violently attacked African-American communities.

It was not just southern leaders that kept African Americans powerless. In 1896, the U.S. Supreme Court ruled that segregation laws keeping African Americans separate from whites were legal. This meant that African Americans were forced to use separate schools, trains, hotels, even restrooms and water fountains. In this case—*Plessy v. Ferguson*—the Court said that segregation had to mean "separate but equal" treatment, but that did not become the practice. African-American facilities were almost always inferior to white facilities. Separate but equal laws would be used for decades to deprive African Americans of basic rights most other Americans took for granted.

The African-American leader Booker T. Washington believed education was the path to blacks being accepted into American society. *(Library of Congress)*

"I shall never permit myself to stoop so low as to hate another man."

—African-American leader Booker T. Washington on racism in the United States

In 1896, the Supreme Court upheld America's segregation laws. In this 1902 segregated school, black students learn about American history.
(Library of Congress)

In some ways, it was even worse for American Indians. As more and more settlers came to the United States throughout the 1800s, American Indians lost their land and homes. In 1830, Congress passed the Indian Removal Act to free land for more white settlers. The law gave the president the authority to move eastern Indian tribes to land west of the Mississippi River. By 1840, the government had forced over 70,000 Indians out of their tribal lands. The removal of the Cherokee from their Georgia homes in 1838–39 was called the Trail of Tears because thousands died of starvation and disease during the forced journey west.

During the second half of the 19th century, there were many battles between American troops and different tribes of American Indians over land west of the Mississippi River. In 1876, the Teton Lakota and Cheyenne defeated General Custer and his troops at the battle of the Little Bighorn in Montana, but it was one of the very few victories for American Indians. Some of the battles were more like massacres. In 1864 at Sand Creek, Colorado, about 300 Cheyenne and Arapaho were killed by U.S. cavalry as they peacefully awaited surrender terms. In 1890 at Wounded Knee in South Dakota, about 200 Lakota Sioux men, women, and children were killed by U.S. soldiers in the last major armed conflict of the Indian Wars.

More than 400 treaties were signed with American Indians as settlers entered tribal lands reserved for Indian tribes. Almost all of them were broken as the settlers needed more and more land. The final straw came in 1887 when Congress passed the Dawes Act, which broke up most tribal lands into smaller pieces of land 40 to 120 acres in size and distributed them to individuals and families. Whatever land was left over after the distribution was sold to white settlers.

The stated intention of the Dawes Act was to help Indians become farmers and be assimilated into white society, but most Indian tribes did not want to give up their traditional way of life for farming and much of the land was not farmable anyway. Gradually, many of the Indians sold off this land cheaply or were cheated out of it by corrupt land speculators and white settlers. By 1900, according to official figures, only about 200,000 American Indians remained in the United States. All of them would not be granted citizenship until 1924.

PRESIDENT McKINLEY IS ASSASSINATED

In 1901, the Progressive movement had many ideas and growing public support. What it lacked was a strong national leader powerful enough to bring about reform. It would take a presidential assassination for that leader to emerge. The 1901 assassination of President William McKinley would be the third presidential assassination the country had seen in 35 years. (Abraham Lincoln had been assassinated in 1865 and James Garfield in 1881.)

In the 1900 election, Americans reelected their popular President William McKinley to a second term. *(Smithsonian Institute)*

Teddy Roosevelt was a sickly child who suffered from asthma and poor eyesight. He overcame his weaknesses by devoting himself to a strenuous life of constant exercise.

"The old laws and the old customs are no longer sufficient."

—Teddy Roosevelt
upon taking office

Spanish-American War hero Theodore Roosevelt became president in 1901 after the assassination of President McKinley. *(Library of Congress)*

In the election of 1900, Americans reelected President McKinley to lead them into the new century. His vice president was New York governor Theodore Roosevelt. On September 6, 1901, McKinley was attending the Pan-American Exposition in Buffalo, New York. As he stood in a reception line shaking hands, he was approached by Leon Czolgosz, a 28-year-old Polish immigrant. Czolgosz was an anarchist, and he had a history of mental illness. As McKinley reached out to shake the assassin's hand, Czolgosz shot him. At first, it looked as though the president would recover, but his condition worsened and he died eight days later on September 14, 1901.

Just six years earlier in 1895, Teddy Roosevelt had been a commissioner on the New York City Police Board. From a wealthy New York family, he was an active and courageous advocate of honesty in public service and social change. As police commissioner, he patrolled the streets at night looking for policemen neglecting their duties. His political rise had been swift, from police commissioner to secretary of the navy to vice president. When McKinley died, Teddy Roosevelt became the youngest president the country had ever had. Roosevelt had been a hero of the Spanish-American War, but many wondered if he was up to the daunting challenges that lay ahead in the new century.

The best-selling book of 1900 was Frank Baum's *The Wonderful Wizard of Oz.*

CHAPTER 2

TEDDY ROOSEVELT TAKES THE HELM, 1901–1904

Roosevelt's promise of a "square deal" for every American made him very popular with the people. *(Library of Congress)*

TEDDY ROOSEVELT WAS NOT ONLY THE youngest president the United States had ever had, he also came from a very different background than previous 19th-century presidents. He was financially well-to-do and well educated. Up to that point in U.S. history, after the era of Presidents Washington, Adams, Jefferson, and Madison had passed, the upper class had looked down on public

For most of his life, Roosevelt read two or three books a day. He also wrote 24 books and more than 150,000 letters during his lifetime.

"We demand that big business give the American people a square deal."

—Teddy Roosevelt on his reasons for trust-busting

While president, Roosevelt and his family kept several pets at the White House including a small bear, a guinea pig, a badger, a blue macaw, a pig, a hen, and a rabbit.

service as something beneath them. Roosevelt's father, however, believed that the rich were obliged to give something back to the society that had given them so much. He also instilled in Teddy the desire to be one of the governing, not the governed.

ROOSEVELT'S BACKGROUND

Roosevelt was born on October 27, 1858, in New York City. His father, Theodore Roosevelt, Sr., was a businessman who traced his Dutch ancestry back to 1649 when Claes van Rosenvelt migrated to America. Roosevelt's mother, Mittie Bulloch, was a southern belle from Georgia. Roosevelt led a privileged childhood surrounded with servants and tutors. He was a good student who loved to read about a variety of subjects, especially natural history, but he was a sickly child. He suffered from weak eyesight and severe asthma, and there were times when the family even feared he might not survive his childhood.

As he grew, Roosevelt overcame his frailty by maintaining a strenuous life of constant exercise including boxing, wrestling, weightlifting, and swimming. He also became a scholar, writing books and graduating from Harvard University in 1880. After graduation, Roosevelt married Alice Hathaway Lee and started his career in politics by winning a seat in the New York State Assembly. As an assemblyman, Roosevelt made a name for himself by fighting corruption. He learned how to work with both parties to get things done, a skill that would also mark his presidency. He served in the state assembly for three years and as chairman of the New York delegation to the Republican National Convention in 1884 until personal tragedy struck.

On February 14, 1884, his wife died giving birth to their daughter, Alice, and his mother died of typhoid fever on the same day. Roosevelt's diary entry for that day was, "The light has gone out of my life." In an attempt to recover from this tragedy, Roosevelt decided to abandon politics and life in the East. He left his daughter in the care of his older sister and traveled West, starting the Elkhorn Ranch in the Dakota Territory. For the next two years, he lived the life of a cowboy and rancher. He hunted buffalo, wrestled calves, and rode horses, sometimes 100 miles a day.

Roosevelt called the two years on his ranch "the romance of my life," but by 1886, he remembered his father's words about public service and returned to New York and politics. He remarried and ran for mayor of New York City. He lost the election but made a name for himself during the 1888 presidential election by campaigning for Republican nominee Benjamin Harrison. During the campaign, Roosevelt spoke about government reform, especially the hiring of government (or civil service) workers based on their skills rather than by the tradition of patronage, or party loyalty. At the time, most government jobs were filled by supporters of the winning party, not necessarily those who were best qualified.

Harrison won the election and rewarded Roosevelt's efforts by appointing him U.S. civil service commissioner in 1889. As commissioner over the next six years, Roosevelt further established his reputation as a progressive, fighting patronage and corruption. He helped reform civil service laws, even challenging the postmaster general, and his fame as a public servant began to spread.

In 1895, Roosevelt returned to New York City to serve as president of the police board. A few years earlier, Roosevelt had read Jacob Riis's exposé of New York poverty, *How the Other Half Lives,* and was deeply affected by the book. Like many other progressives at the time, he felt he might have a bigger impact at the city level where many government reforms were needed. As president of the police board, Roosevelt patrolled the streets making sure the police were doing their job.

TEDDY BEARS ARE BORN

Theodore Roosevelt loved to hunt. In 1902, he was hunting in Mississippi when he came upon a trapped bear cub. Roosevelt's hosts had trapped the cub so that he could have a trophy to take home. Roosevelt, however, refused to shoot the helpless animal. The following year, a toy manufacturer in New York made a stuffed bear with button eyes and called it "Teddy's Bear." It became the most popular toy of its day, and teddy bears remain popular to this day.

(National Archives)

On a hunting trip to Africa after his presidency, Roosevelt killed more than 296 animals including lions, elephants, and water buffaloes.

> **Roosevelt's cavalry unit in Cuba during the Spanish-American War was known as the Rough Riders.**

He also broke up alliances between criminals and police and instituted the law that closed saloons on Sundays to cut down on crime.

By 1897, Roosevelt was eager to become involved in national affairs again, and he felt that the U.S. military, especially its navy, needed strengthening. He asked some influential friends he had in Washington to help him be appointed assistant secretary of the navy under the new president, William McKinley. He won the

Roosevelt led his Rough Riders to victory at the Battle of San Juan Hill and became a national hero. *(National Archives)*

appointment and spent the next year building the navy for the war he saw coming against Spain in Cuba. After the sinking of the battleship *Maine,* President McKinley declared war on Spain on April 25, 1898. One month later, Roosevelt resigned his post as assistant secretary of the navy and put together his troop of Rough Riders from his old cowboy and socialite friends. On July 1, his charge at the Battle of San Juan Hill in Cuba made him a national hero.

When Roosevelt returned home after the war, the Republican party asked him to run for governor of New York. He won the election, but over the next two years, Roosevelt made enemies within his party. Many party leaders did not agree with his views on government reforms, and they feared his independent attitude. To get rid of him, the party leaders convinced President McKinley to choose Roosevelt as his vice-presidential running mate in the 1900 election. The McKinley-Roosevelt team was very popular and won the election easily, but any party leaders who thought they were getting rid of Roosevelt were mistaken. Less than one year later, after McKinley's assassination in September 1901, Roosevelt was president.

Roosevelt would be reelected easily in 1904, and during his two terms, Roosevelt expanded the powers of the presidency as no other president had before. His time in office set the standard for U.S. presidents for the rest of the 20th century.

DOMESTIC AFFAIRS AND ECONOMICS

After taking office, Roosevelt promised to continue on the course McKinley had set for his second term. As a progressive, however, he also promised every American a "square deal." In February 1902, he chose his first battle—the trusts of big business. He also fought for the rights of workers, for dependable financial markets, and for clear standards for the purity of food and medicines.

President McKinley was the first president to have to deal with the issue of imperialism vs. isolationism. He chose imperialism.
(Library of Congress)

In 1902, the U.S. Army changed the color of its uniform from blue to green. The blue uniform had proved too good a target during the Spanish-American War.

The popular soft drink, Coca Cola, derived its name from one of its ingredients, cocaine. In 1903, the soda company decided to substitute caffeine for the cocaine.

Trust-Busting

As industrialization swept across America at the end of the 19th century and beginning of the 20th century, big business grew. To increase their power and profits even more, the bigger companies eliminated competition by buying out the smaller companies. For example, in 1880 there were more than 1,000 steel companies in the United States By 1900, the formation of trusts had reduced that number to 70. In 1901, Andrew Carnegie formed a trust, made up of what companies remained, and named it U.S. Steel. Since U.S. Steel no longer had any competition, Carnegie could set steel prices as high as he wished and workers' wages as low as he wished.

The same practice was creating monopolies all of America's big businesses. By 1902, J. D. Rockefeller's Standard Oil controlled 85 percent of the oil industry. Six trusts controlled 95 percent of America's railroads. Trusts accounted for just 1 percent of the companies in the country but they controlled 40 percent of the production.

The Sherman Anti-trust Act had been passed in 1890 to control monopolies as being against the public interest, but the law had never been enforced. In 1902, Roosevelt told his attorney general, Philander Knox, to use the Sherman Act against J.P. Morgan's huge Northern Securities railroad trust. The big business world was shocked because the federal government had never tried to intervene in their affairs before. In fact, in 1895, Morgan had prevented a financial crisis for the government of President Grover Cleveland by loaning $65 million in gold to the government.

Morgan was outraged when he heard of Roosevelt's intention to dissolve his company. He met with Roosevelt at the White House and told the president, "If we have done anything wrong, send your man to my man and they can fix it up," but the fix Roosevelt wanted was the breakup of the trust. The case eventually reached the Supreme Court in 1904 and Roosevelt won. The court ordered Northern Securities to be dissolved.

MOTHER JONES AND THE CHILDREN'S MARCH ON WASHINGTON

There were many labor leaders during the 1900s, but there were none quite like Mother Jones. When she was a young woman living in Memphis, Tennessee, all four of her sons and her husband died of malaria. She moved to Chicago and opened a very successful dressmaking shop but it burned down in the great Chicago fire of 1871.

These personal tragedies gave Mother Jones great compassion for her fellow humans. She decided to spend the rest of her life working for labor rights. Her most famous crusade came in Philadelphia in 1903 when 75,000 textile workers, including 10,000 children, walked off the job. Many of the children had already been crippled by accidents in the workplace. Mother Jones said, "Philadelphia's mansions were built on the broken bones, the quivering hearts, and drooping heads of these children."

Mother Jones marched the children to Washington to try to see President Roosevelt. When he refused to see them, Jones took the children to New York City. She held a huge rally there protesting the lack of regulations concerning child labor. The Pennsylvania legislature eventually passed a bill prohibiting children under 14 from working in factories. Mother Jones spent the rest of her life speaking out for workers' rights. She died in 1930 at the age of 100.

Mother Jones was a leader in the battle against child labor. This poster urged other Americans to join the fight. *(Library of Congress)*

Cramped and unsanitary tenement life drove many immigrants west. There, conditions might be harsh, but not as harsh as for this young girl bathing in a sink. *(Lewis Hine/George Eastman House)*

"They don't suffer. Why, they can't even speak English."

—Mine-owner representative George Baer when asked about the horrible working conditions of the coal miners

In 1901, J. P. Morgan bought U.S. Steel from Andrew Carnegie for $492 million. The new trust, U.S. Steel Corp., was worth $1.4 billion, the first billion-dollar corporation in history.

"Business run in this way loses all its sportsmanlike qualities. It is fit only for tricksters."

—Writer Ida Tarbell describing the business practices of robber baron John D. Rockefeller

Roosevelt's trust-busting was very popular with the American public. The promise of a square deal seemed to be coming true. In all, Roosevelt initiated 44 antitrust suits and Congress pursued many others, including one against Rockefeller's Standard Oil, which was finally dissolved in 1911. Roosevelt also gave greater powers to the Interstate Commerce Commission to administer laws regarding business. In 1905, the Hepburn Act gave the agency the power to regulate the railroads.

Labor and Reform

Roosevelt also took an active role in the growing number of disputes between labor and management. In May 1902, 150,000 coal workers went out on strike demanding a 20 percent pay raise, a nine-hour workday, and recognition of their union. Resolution of the strike was vital because coal was the country's most important fuel at the time. It heated most of America's homes, schools, and hospitals. A disastrous coal shortage was possible if the strike dragged on into winter.

As winter approached, there was no resolution mainly because the mine owners refused to negotiate. Once again, Roosevelt decided it was in the public interest to intervene and he became the first president to help settle a labor dispute. He invited the two sides to the White House, where the mine owners still refused to negotiate. Roosevelt was so upset at the owners he threatened to send U.S. Army troops to operate the mines.

Help came from an unexpected source as J.P. Morgan convinced the owners to agree to arbitration, or settlement by an uninvolved person or group. Roosevelt set up a commission to study the dispute and the workers went back to work. The following year, the commission granted workers a 10 percent pay raise and a nine-hour workday. The commission did not force the mine owners to recognize the workers' union, but it did set up a conciliation board to hear workers' complaints, and union representatives were included on the board. The decision was a great victory for the progressive movement and made Roosevelt more popular than ever.

With Roosevelt's encouragement, city and state governments also worked on reform laws. Cities started replacing corrupt mayors with commissions. The commissions were found to be much more efficient and honest because power was divided among several people instead of being in the hands of just one person. At the state level, people started voting on important political decisions themselves as referendums began to be placed on the ballot on election day. Starting with Mississippi in 1902, states started using the direct primary to elect their candidates rather than having powerful and often corrupt party leaders choose someone. In direct primaries, members of one party vote for the candidate they want to run in the next election. Democrats vote for the person whom they wish to be the Democratic candidate; Republicans vote for the Republican candidate. In the 19th century, regular Democrats and Republicans often had to just accept whomever party leaders would pick as the candidate. Direct primaries brought more political power to regular party members.

Two stuffed passenger pigeons, which became extinct in 1915, were preserved at the Chicago Academy of Sciences. *(Library of Congress)*

CONSERVATION AND THE WEST

From its beginnings, the United States placed a great deal of hope in its frontier, the vast undeveloped lands west of the Mississippi. Its space and resources were thought to be unlimited. Thomas Jefferson said that America had room enough for "a thousand generations," but the country grew quickly. By 1890 the U.S. Census Bureau declared that the frontier was gone. Unfortunately, not only had the West been settled, much of it had also been destroyed.

Many animal species found only in the American West, such as the passenger pigeon, were wiped out by hunters. The last passenger pigeon died in 1915,

Yosemite National Park in California is famous for its huge sequoia trees. The park was originally protected by President Lincoln in 1864. *(National Archives)*

although flocks of millions of passenger pigeons once were common. Between 1800 and 1890, the U.S. bison population dropped from 60 million to under 1,000. Mining companies had stripped mountains of valuable ore leaving the land barren and worthless. Foresters had destroyed millions of acres of forests, including huge and ancient sequoias, without replanting for the future.

The conservation of America's land and resources was a new idea in Roosevelt's time. Previous presidents had made only a few efforts. In 1864, Abraham Lincoln granted the Yosemite Valley to California, but only on the condition that it "be held for public use, resort, and recreation for all time." In 1872, Ulysses S. Grant signed a bill passed by Congress placing 1 million acres of Montana and Wyoming known as Yellowstone under federal control. It forbid settlers from moving into the area and created America's first national park. In 1890, Benjamin Harrison established the Sequoia National Park in

JOHN MUIR, AMERICA'S FIRST CONSERVATIONIST

Long before President Roosevelt signed his conservation acts in the early 1900s, John Muir was speaking out for the preservation of American forests and resources. In 1867, when Muir was 29, he left his factory job in Indiana and set out on a thousand-mile walk to the Gulf of Mexico through America's forests. The following year, he headed west and wound up in California's Yosemite Valley.

The destruction of nature he saw along the way appalled Muir. He settled in the Yosemite area and started to speak out on preservation issues. In his lifetime, he would publish nearly 300 articles and 10 major books, and his writing helped build pub-lic support for the conservation of U.S. forests. His first success came in 1890 when President Harrison signed a bill establishing the Yosemite and Sequoia National Parks. In 1892, Muir started the Sierra Club to protect Yosemite and Sequoia and campaign for more national parks.

Muir continued to live in the woods until his death in 1914. He raised money for his cause by acting as a guide for wealthy travelers who came to Yosemite for vacation. When President Roosevelt visited Yosemite in 1903, Muir was his guide. Roosevelt called it "the bulliest day of my life" and the two remained lifelong friends.

"Any fool can destroy trees; they cannot run away."

—Conservationist John Muir, founder of the Sierra Club

California, but the destruction of America's land continued to proceed much faster than the preservation.

Roosevelt was outraged at the destruction of the country's resources and vowed to correct the problem. The battle was not easy because there were powerful business interests, especially in the West, who viewed the resources simply as means to make financial profit. These businesses had many supporters in Congress who tried to block Roosevelt's conservation bills. Roosevelt once again expanded his presidential powers and often simply declared an act of conservation by proclamation.

Roosevelt's main ally in his conservation efforts was Gifford Pinchot, head of the federal government's Forest Service. Pinchot believed that federal land should serve "the greatest number." This moderate view combined preservation with the controlled use of resources as necessary and with conditions. For example, lumber

The beautiful scenery of Yellowstone National Park extends over Wyoming, Montana, and Idaho. It became America's first national park in 1872.
(*U.S. Geological Survey*)

was essential to build houses, so loggers should be allowed to clear a certain amount of a forest as long as they reseeded and maintained the cleared area. Because people needed electricity, dams should be built to produce hydroelectric power, but only with government control. Pinchot's attitude of compromise was shared by Roosevelt and resulted in Roosevelt's success in getting many of his programs enacted.

Roosevelt's conservation programs covered several different areas. During his administration, nearly 150 million acres of land were set aside as either national forests or national parks, which forms about 50 percent of the current U.S. system. He proclaimed nine places as national monuments including Devil's Tower in Wyoming, the Petrified Forest and Grand Canyon in

MAN VS. NATURE: GALVESTON, TEXAS

Two of the biggest disasters ever to hit the United States happened in the 1900s. One was the San Francisco earthquake in 1906, which killed more than 700 people. The other was the hurricane that hit the island city of Galveston, Texas, on September 7, 1900. When the storm moved in that Labor Day weekend, Galveston was filled with tourists. At that time, there was no way to warn residents about storms in advance, so they had no time to prepare or escape.

The hurricane brought very heavy rain and winds of more than 100 mph. Tidal waves continuously washed over the city, destroying telegraph poles, homes, and the bridges linking Galveston to the mainland. After the storm passed, the survivors wandered the streets amazed at the damage they saw. In one section four blocks wide and three miles long, every house and building had been destroyed. The hurricane left 6,000 people dead, 5,000 injured, and 10,000 homeless. In terms of loss of life, it is still the worst natural disaster to ever hit America.

Arizona, and Natural Bridges in Utah. Roosevelt created the first wildlife refuges to protect endangered species and habitats. The first refuge Roosevelt established was Pelican Island in Florida, protecting hundreds of species of birds, fish, plants, and animals.

Roosevelt did not believe in simply preserving America's West and controlling use of its natural resources. He also wanted the land settled by homesteaders, especially the vast expanses of dry land. Roosevelt agreed with those who saw several benefits to the country from this huge settlement program. First, the East's cities were overpopulated. It was hoped that homesteading might relieve urban congestion and poverty. Second, if the land were properly irrigated, it could grow food and raise cattle for a growing population that needed more food. As the area became populated, it would also help the railroad business and complete the transcontinental railroad system.

The settlement program started with the Reclamation Act of 1902, which required that all

In 1903, E. T. Fitch and M. C. Krarup made the first successful coast-to-coast automobile trip. It took them 52 days, and the public was amazed at their speed.

The contrast between life in urban eastern tenements and on the wide-open prairie was stark. For city dwellers used to buying hot potatoes from street vendors, the work required to prepare a meal could be a shock. *(Library of Congress)*

When Roosevelt was a cowboy in the Dakotas, he once captured three thieves and spent six days escorting them back to the local sheriff.

money raised from the sale of government-owned lands be used on irrigation projects in the West. Over the following decade, the government spent more than $70 million on electrical and water projects. Many of the West's dams, including Roosevelt Dam outside Phoenix, Arizona, were built under this act. The new irrigation turned dry desert land into fertile farmland. As a result, more settlers took advantage of the Homestead Act of 1862, which granted up to 160 acres of land in return for maintaining it for five years.

Roosevelt's conservation and reclamation programs were a huge success and lived up to Pinchot's idea of land serving "the greatest number." New farmers in the West also had the advantage of new farming methods and new technology. The steam tractor and gas tractor replaced the horse as the most common form of farm power. More land could be cultivated much more quickly. The result was a golden age of farming from 1900 to 1920 that saw farm prices rise 72 percent.

FOREIGN POLICY: "SPEAK SOFTLY"

After the United States gained control of several colonies after the Spanish-American War in 1898, a debate started in the country between isolationists and imperialists. The isolationists believed the United States should grant the colonies their freedom and concentrate on problems within the United States. They argued that the United States had been founded on the principle of freedom from outside control and that the new colonies deserved the same freedom. The imperialists believed the United States should keep the colonies and use its power to control events around the world. Some imperialists even thought the United States should use its military power to gain more colonies and expand world influence. Some of these more extreme imperialists

This political cartoon from 1904 pokes fun at Roosevelt's foreign policy of "Speak softly and carry a big stick." *(Library of Congress)*

On the Fourth of July, 1903, President Roosevelt sent the first around-the-world message using the recently completed Pacific telegraph cable. The message took 12 minutes to go around the world and reach him again.

"The White House is a bully pulpit!"

—Teddy Roosevelt on the joys of being president

believed in manifest destiny, the idea that Americans were superior and had been chosen by God to bring the American way of life to others around the world.

Roosevelt was an imperialist. His motto in foreign policy was "speak softly and carry a big stick," but he had no intention of acquiring new colonies. He wanted treaties with nations that would help U.S. businesses. With farming and industry booming, the United States had many goods available for sale and trade. Roosevelt believed America's influence in markets around the world was essential to its economy. His big stick was a strong military and he threatened to use it several times over his two terms, but he never did. He was a very effective negotiator and always managed to get what he wanted without war.

Roosevelt's first test came in 1903 when a dispute arose between the United States and England over the border between Canada and Alaska, an U.S. territory at the time. The area had become important because of a recent discovery of gold along the border. Roosevelt used both diplomacy and his big stick to settle the issue. He had his Secretary of State John Hay set up a tribunal with three U.S. representatives and three British representatives to determine the correct boundary. He also said that if the tribunal did not find in favor of the United States, he would send in troops and occupy the area anyway. The tribunal found in favor of the U.S. claim.

Another test of Roosevelt's foreign policy came that same year in Venezuela. Germany set up a naval blockade of Venezuela in an effort to collect a long overdue debt of $40 million. Roosevelt ordered an U.S. naval fleet to the Caribbean and told Germany he would use force if they tried to acquire any territory in their dispute with Venezuela. Germany removed the blockade, and the issue was settled by a world tribunal that granted Germany $8 million and ruled it improper to use force to collect debts.

TYPHOID MARY

Mary Mallon was an Irish immigrant who came to the United States in the 1890s and worked as a cook. Around 1900, she caught typhoid fever. She recovered and went back to work in the kitchen for wealthy families in Long Island. The problem was that even though she had recovered, she still spread the disease of typhoid. Handling food was an easy way to transmit the bacteria that caused the disease.

Family members from almost every family she worked for came down with the disease. There were at least 53 cases of typhoid on Long Island, three of them ending in death. Mallon did not believe she was the cause because she felt fine. Although suspicion fell on her, she escaped to upstate New York. In 1903, there was an outbreak of typhoid in Ithaca, New York, with at least 1,400 cases, and it was discovered that Mallon had been working there. In the next few years, there were four more outbreaks of typhoid in New York State. A health worker traced the origin of each outbreak to Mallon, who became known as Typhoid Mary.

In 1907, the state tracked her down and imprisoned her in a New York City hospital as a threat to public health. She was released in 1910 on the condition that she not work as a cook. In 1914, she was located, again working as a cook. It was probably the only job she knew how to do. Typhoid Mary was imprisoned in the hospital again, this time until her death in 1938.

This diplomatic victory by Roosevelt led to a policy known as the Roosevelt Corollary to the Monroe Doctrine. The Monroe Doctrine of 1823 stated that European countries had no right to interfere in the affairs of any country in North or South America. It was not a law, but U.S. presidents since Monroe had used it as a policy to keep European influence out of the Americas. Roosevelt added one more detail to the policy in 1904. He said that no nation had the right to interfere in the internal affairs of any nation in the Americas unless that nation was threatening "the ties of civilized society." In that case, he said, only the United States had the right to intervene and ensure the region's peace and stability.

CIVIL RIGHTS

One of the first things President Roosevelt did after he took office in 1901 was invite educator Booker T. Washington to dinner. He was the first black leader ever invited to the White House. Racism was still so prevalent in America, especially in the South, that this simple act resulted in white riots in several southern cities. Despite Roosevelt's gesture toward Washington, his

Booker T. Washington (seated second from left) founded the National Negro Business League in 1901 to promote African Americans in the business world. *(Library of Congress)*

square deal did little to improve the lives of minorities. There were few gains in civil rights during the 1900s, but there were some noted developments.

For the most part, conditions worsened for African Americans, 80 percent of whom still lived in the South. The 1896 *Plessy v. Ferguson* decision approving of segregation empowered many southern states to create separate and very unequal conditions. The one bright spot during this time was the drop in illiteracy among African Americans, from 45 percent in 1900 to 30 percent in 1910. The drop was probably due to Washington's call to African Americans to educate themselves.

Washington felt that if blacks bettered themselves through education and self-reliance, white society would then accept them. As a result, many black communities built new schools. Still, segregationists wanted to prevent blacks from being accepted into white society. As blacks tried harder to enter white society, violence against them increased. Their schools and churches were burned and lynchings, hangings without a trial, were common. Some historians estimate as many as 1,000 lynchings occurred from 1900 to 1910.

While Washington called on African Americans to accept their position until education brought them acceptance, another black leader called for a different approach. Unlike Washington, W. E. B. DuBois was a northern black, born and educated in Massachusetts. He was the first black to receive a Ph.D. from Harvard University. DuBois felt blacks would never win their rights and political power through education alone. He said blacks must be active in demanding their rights from white society. He said, if necessary, legal action must be initiated to obtain decent schools, voting rights, and fair-paying jobs.

After years of researching the history and plight of the African American, DuBois published his findings and beliefs in *The Souls of Black Folk* in 1903. In this book, DuBois writes of the conflict of African Americans feeling both American and black, "haunted by the ghost of an untrue dream." He wrote, "The history of the American Negro is the history of strife" and asserted they could no longer just wait for their place in U.S. society. The book attracted a lot of attention among both blacks and whites, but little changed.

"We claim for ourselves every single right that belongs to a freeborn American and until we get these rights, we will never cease to protest and assail the ears of America."

—W. E. B. DuBois at the Harper's Ferry, Virginia, conference on black civil rights

SHEET MUSIC

Since many families owned a piano at the turn of the century, all they needed to provide an evening of entertainment was sheet music. Sales of sheet music soared during the 1900s with nearly 100 songs selling more than a million copies. The top seller was "In the Shade of the Old Apple Tree" which sold 8 million copies.

To keep up with the demand for sheet music, songwriters of the era started cranking out new songs by the thousands. One area of New York City became known as Tin Pan Alley because of the sound of all the

Sheet music was a big part of popular culture. Popular songs spread by means of sheet music rather than by radio or recordings, and many had patriotic themes. *(New York Public Library)*

songwriters composing their songs for the sheet music publishers. One Tin Pan Alley songwriter, Van Tilzer, wrote more than 2,000 songs for Tin Pan Alley publishers, but the most famous writers to come out of the era were Irving Berlin and George M. Cohan.

As sheet music spread popular songs around the country, an American style of music began to evolve. This development would become more obvious in the 1910s as recorded music replaced sheet music in popularity. Besides the popular songs of Tin Pan Alley, other musical styles were evolving in the South, particularly around New Orleans.

CHAPTER 3

ROOSEVELT'S SECOND TERM, 1905–1908

ROOSEVELT WAS VERY POPULAR AND WON the presidential election of 1904, easily defeating the Democratic candidate Alton B. Parker of New York. Roosevelt won 56.4 percent of the popular vote and 336 electoral votes, while Parker got 37.6 of the popular vote and only 140 electoral votes. However, nearly 5 percent of Americans voted for either Socialist Eugene Debs or the Prohibition candidate, Silas Swallow. The forces supporting Prohibition were small, but by 1919, their influence would affect the United States profoundly.

The Panama Canal was an engineering marvel because of its huge locks—dams with gates that permitted water levels to be raised and lowered as ships passed through. *(Library of Congress)*

A palindrome is a word or phrase that is the same spelled backward as it is forward. A famous palindrome coined during Roosevelt's presidency was "a man, a plan, a canal, Panama."

SUCCESS OVERSEAS

Roosevelt's foreign policy brought him several diplomatic victories during his second term. In 1905, he negotiated the Treaty of Portsmouth, which resolved the Russo-Japanese War of 1904–05. He won the Nobel Peace Prize as a result. (Roosevelt donated the money from this award to the American people.) In 1906, Roosevelt sent a delegate to resolve a dispute between France and Germany over trade influence in Morocco. In 1907, his Gentlemen's Agreement with Japan settled an immigration dispute in California.

In 1907, Roosevelt also sent his Great White Fleet on a year-long voyage around the world. The fleet was the pride of Roosevelt's new navy—sixteen new powerful battleships all painted white. It was supposed to be a goodwill mission, but Roosevelt was also showing off his big stick policy of intimidation, especially to Japan, whose military posed a threat to America's new presence in the Pacific. The voyage was a success. By the time the fleet had returned home, Japan had agreed not to interfere with America's affairs in the Pacific. In return, the United States agreed to not interfere in Japan's occupation of Korea.

The greatest accomplishment of Roosevelt's foreign policy, however, was the building of the Panama Canal, which began as Roosevelt's second term started. Since the completion of the Suez Canal in Egypt in 1869, U.S. business and shipping interests had wondered if a similar canal could be built through Central America connecting the Atlantic and Pacific Oceans. Such a canal would cut the sea route from New York to San Francisco from 13,000 miles around South America to just 5,200 miles, making the transport of goods to and from the West Coast much cheaper and quicker.

As the United States became a world military and economic power with interests in the Pacific, the canal became even more important. A French company led by Ferdinand de Lesseps, the builder of the Suez Canal, had tried to build a canal through the 50-mile-wide isthmus of Panama from 1882 to 1888. The attempt failed as de Lesseps faced engineering problems, bankruptcy, and tropical diseases such as malaria and yellow fever. More than 5,500 workers died during the six years, most from these diseases.

In 1900, an American researcher, Dr. Walter Reed, discovered that yellow fever and many other tropical diseases were spread by mosquitos. If the mosquito population in an area is wiped out, the diseases disappear. Roosevelt felt confident that the canal could be built. He signed a treaty with the president of Colombia, the country that owned the Panama isthmus, giving the United States control of a six-mile strip of land. In exchange, Colombia would receive $10 million and annual payments of $250,000.

The Colombian senate, however, unanimously vetoed the deal and demanded more money. Roosevelt was furious and considered sending in troops to take Panama, but he had another ally who settled the conflict for him. The Panamanians had been fighting for their independence for years, and they decided it might be a good time to try again. Roosevelt aided the revolt by having U.S. ships prevent Colombian soldiers from reaching the area. In 1903, Panama won its independence and immediately accepted Roosevelt's offer, granting the United States a ten-mile strip of land called the Canal Zone.

Construction of the canal began in 1904. Roosevelt kept a close eye on every detail and even visited the site in 1906, becoming the first president to ever leave the United States while in office. The canal became an engineering marvel because of its use of locks. Locks are dams with gates that open and close to raise or lower ships to different levels. The locks were necessary because sea level is different on the Atlantic and Pacific sides of Panama. It took 50,000 workers, ten years, and $350 million to complete the Panama Canal.

Roosevelt extended his conservation efforts with the Antiquities Act of 1906, which protected sites that were of historical or archaeological value, such as deserted mining towns, known as ghost towns, and Native American burial grounds.

By the turn of the century, white settlers had taken over most Indian land. Here, a young Hopi Indian woman grinds corn ca. 1909.
(National Archives)

African-American leader W. E. B. DuBois believed legal action, not education, was the best way to achieve equality for blacks in America. *(Library of Congress)*

To Roosevelt and many others, it was his greatest accomplishment, but he was also criticized for how he acquired the Canal Zone. He defended himself with his usual frankness. "I took the Canal Zone and let Congress debate," he said, "and while the debate goes on, the canal does also." In 1921, Congress would award Colombia $20 million compensation for the United States's handling of the affair.

CIVIL RIGHTS

The beginning of organized African-American civil rights activity is often attributed to W. E. B. DuBois and the Niagara Movement, which DuBois started in 1905. That year he and 28 other black leaders met at Niagara Falls to discuss segregation and black civil rights. The group was forced to meet on the Canadian side of the falls after no U.S. hotel would admit them. The leaders put together a list of demands including equal education, an end to segregation, and a reversal of the *Plessy v. Ferguson* decision.

Groups such as the National American Woman Suffrage Association, shown on the right, had worked for a woman's right to vote since 1848. *(Library of Congress)*

The Niagara Movement is often considered the beginning of the black civil rights movement in America. W. E. B DuBois appears second from right, middle row. *(Schomburg Center, New York Public Library)*

In 1908, the residents of Springfield, Illinois, Abraham Lincoln's hometown, attempted to remove all of the town's black residents. The resulting riot convinced many in the Niagara Movement that a new group was needed. In 1909, the group expanded to include whites and became the NAACP, the National Association for the Advancement of Colored People, which became the most influential group in the fight for civil rights during the 20th century.

The women's movement continued to make small gains throughout the 1900s. More states were finally granting women such basic rights as the right to own property, to claim all their earnings, to share equally in the custody of their children, and to have access to higher education. These were all rights that had been demanded more than 50 years earlier at the first women's rights convention in Seneca Falls, New York, in 1848. However, women still did not have another right demanded at that convention: the right to vote. In the 1900s, suffragists, or those in favor of voting rights, realized the only way to achieve their voting rights would be through a constitutional amendment. Their work for this amendment would finally succeed in 1920.

On August 13–14, 1906, a shooting spree in Brownsville, Texas, left one white civilian dead. Locals accused black soldiers from a nearby army camp of the crime. President Roosevelt dishonorably discharged 167 blacks from the camp even though they denied the charge and there was no proof against them.

"No sensible woman wants to vote."

—Former president Grover Cleveland on the woman's suffrage debate

In 1907, the first underarm deodorant was offered for sale to women. The product, Ovorono, was not marketed to men because, at the time, men were expected to smell as nature intended.

TECHNOLOGICAL ADVANCES: THE AUTOMOBILE AGE

Important innovations during the 1900s include air conditioning, invented by Willis Carrier in 1902, and the vacuum cleaner, invented by James Spangler in 1908. However, the real technology boom took place in transportation. The railroad system continued to expand as homesteaders settled the West. By 1908 the United States had more than 200,000 miles of track, the most of any country in the world. In 1903, the Wright Brothers achieved the first successful flight of a heavier-than-air craft, but few took notice of the achievement until the army became interested in 1908. As cities continued to grow, trolley systems expanded. By the end of the decade, there were more than 20,000 miles of trolley routes in the United States. Almost all of them were electric.

The 1900s was the start of America's auto age. In 1900, there were only 8,000 cars registered in the United States. By 1910, there were nearly half a million. One reason for the boom was technological improvements. Manufacturers of rubber tires, such as Goodyear, made

Many of America's great car-making companies started early. To the right is a 1903 Buick, a popular model.
(Buick Motor Division)

The Ford Model T was born in 1908. Its widespread adoption was due to its price. Mass production would eventually make it affordable to most American families. From $825 in 1908, the car's price eventually went as low as $280. *(Ford Motor Company)*

tremendous advances, and automobiles had far fewer flats than before. Steering wheels replaced tillers and gave drivers more control. Electric starters replaced the manual crank and made starting much easier. The muffler made autos quieter and gradually roads improved.

Throughout the 1900s, autos were still pretty expensive, but one businessman was about to change that. In 1903, Henry Ford started the Ford Motor Company. He said he wanted to "build a motor car for the great multitude." He thought he could do this by use of assembly line production of his autos where they would all "come through the factory just alike." In 1908, he introduced his Model T at a cost of $825. The price was still too high, and Ford sold only 11,000 Model T's in 1908 and 1909. He would soon make improvements in his assembly line, however, and revolutionize auto production.

SPORTS IN THE SPOTLIGHT

In the early 20th century, there was a tremendous increase in the popularity of spectator sports such as baseball, football, and boxing. One reason for this was Teddy Roosevelt's belief in athletics and the "strenuous life," as he referred to it. Roosevelt's popularity

"In life, as in a football game, the principle is to hit the line hard, don't foul and don't shirk, but hit the line hard."

—Teddy Roosevelt describing his philosophy of football and life

The Carlisle Indian School was a boarding school for American Indian children who were taken away from their parents' homes. *(Library of Congress)*

THE GREATEST ATHLETE OF THE 20TH CENTURY

In a poll of American sports writers in 1950, Jim Thorpe was voted the "greatest athlete of the century." In similar polls at the end of the century, Thorpe consistently placed at or near the top. What sets Thorpe apart from other athletes of the century is that he excelled at so many different sports. He was also forced to endure one of the great humiliations in sports history.

Thorpe, half American Indian, started his amazing athletic career as a collegiate football star at Carlisle Indian School. In 1911 and 1912, Thorpe won All-American honors and led his unknown school to victories over powerhouse programs such as Harvard, Army, and the University of Pennsylvania. Also, in 1912, Thorpe won the gold medal in both the pentathlon and decathlon at the Summer Olympics in Stockholm, Sweden. The two events include 15 track and field events measuring speed, strength, and endurance.

After college, from 1915 to 1929, Thorpe helped popularize professional football with his tremendous ability as a running back. In 1920, he served as president of the first professional league, the American Professional Football Association, which later became today's National Football League. Thorpe also played professional baseball from 1913 to 1919, but it was his experience as a semi-pro baseball player from 1909 to 1911 that led to his being stripped of his Olympic gold medals.

When the International Olympic Committee (IOC) discovered in 1913 that Thorpe had been paid for playing semi-pro baseball, a common summer job for college athletes at the time, they decided he was not an amateur athlete and should not have participated in the 1912 Olympics. They took away his medals and forbid him from competing in future Olympics. The medals were restored to his family in 1982, 29 years after his death.

made him a role model for many Americans. They may not have been able to keep up with his level of activity, but at the very least he made them interested in athletics.

Football

One of Roosevelt's favorite sports was football and the game became very popular on college campuses during his presidency. Originally, the game was played with no padding, and serious injuries and even deaths among the college players were common. In 1905, Roosevelt persuaded a group of college presidents to draw up new rules to cut down on the brutality of the game. The rule changes, including the introduction of the forward pass, were successful, and attendance rose steadily throughout the 1900s.

Many colleges built new stadiums to handle the increased interest—the Yale Bowl was built in 1914 and held 60,000 fans. In 1915, the Rose Bowl became the first annual game that pitted two of the country's top teams against each other. Most years, teams such as Harvard, Yale, Penn, Army, and Michigan dominated, but one of the biggest upsets in the history of sports took place in 1911. Powerhouse Harvard was defeated by a tiny Pennsylvania school called Carlisle Indian School. Their team was led by their running back and kicker named Jim Thorpe, an American Indian and the best football player of the era.

Boxing

Boxing was also becoming very popular in the early decades of the century. A recent rule change that required boxers to fight with padded gloves rather than bare knuckles made the sport appeal to a wider audience. The heavyweight champion at the start of the century was Jim Jeffries, who retired in 1905 because he

Jim Thorpe was half American Indian. His original Indian name was *Wa-tho-huck,* meaning "bright path."

Jim Thorpe joined the Carlisle Indian School football team in 1907, playing for legendary coach Pop Warner. *(Library of Congress)*

On November 16, 1907, Oklahoma became the 46th state of the union.

had defeated all challengers. A Canadian, Tommy Burns, became the champ, but he was not the best boxer in the world.

The best was a black man, Jack Johnson, who used a more scientific approach to boxing than other fighters of the time. Johnson took on all the best fighters and beat them all. He wanted a shot at Burns's title, but Burns would not fight him because he was black. Johnson started following Burns all around the world—to England, France, and Australia—demanding a fight. Burns finally gave in, and on December 26, 1908, in Sydney, Australia, Johnson beat him easily to win the crown. A huge outcry greeted his return to the United States.

Johnson was a very controversial champion. He was very outspoken about his abilities and would taunt his weaker opponents in the ring. He dared the white boxing world to find a white man who could beat him. They tried for years but Johnson beat all of them. Finally, the ex-champ, Jeffries, was persuaded to come out of retirement. The press called Jeffries the "Great White Hope" and the two fought on July 4, 1910, in Reno, Nevada, in the biggest fight of the era.

THE SAN FRANCISCO EARTHQUAKE

On April 18, 1906, a powerful earthquake hit the San Francisco area of California. The quake toppled buildings and buckled streets. Gas lines crumbled, producing huge fires throughout the city. There was no water to try to put the fires out because the quake broke most of the water pipes. The quake only lasted for about 1 minute, but the fires spread and burned out of control for several days. At its peak it covered 500 square blocks and witnesses claimed the flames stretched a mile into the sky.

The overall damage from the quake was staggering. Twenty-five thousand buildings collapsed or burned, 700 people were dead, and a quarter of a million were homeless. President Roosevelt asked Congress for $2.5 million to help rebuild the area, but San Francisco authorities turned down offers of help from other countries. They said they wanted to show that Americans could take care of themselves.

Johnson again won easily, knocking Jeffries out in the 15th round. It was the high point of Johnson's career and black Americans rejoiced in a pride few had ever known in their lives. Johnson's victory also resulted in violence against African Americans across the nation. Race riots in several American cities left 13 African Americans dead and hundreds injured. The public outcry even included a ban on showing films of the fight. Johnson was so harassed that he moved to Europe. He was finally defeated by Jess Willard in 1915, but he had made his point—he was a great champion and he had broken the color line in boxing.

THE PANIC OF 1907

Throughout Roosevelt's presidency, the U.S. economy flourished—until the panic of 1907. Partly as a result of Roosevelt's prosecution of the oil and railroad trusts, many investors held on to their money, rather than investing it in business. Many companies found themselves short of cash as investors stayed away. By October, more than 8,000 companies had gone bankrupt. The lack of cash in the market created a panic on Wall Street, and stock prices fell dangerously low. Several of New York City's largest banks failed, and the city itself was on the brink of default, which meant that it would not be able to pay back money it had borrowed.

Roosevelt once again needed the astute business mind of J. P. Morgan to prevent a national depression. Morgan persuaded fellow businessmen throughout New York City to loan $25 million to the banks and trusts that were in trouble. The federal government also deposited $25 million in city banks. Morgan had saved the day, but the nation needed a law that would help prevent such financial panics in the future. The following year, Roosevelt signed the Currency Act of 1908. The law gave banks the right to issue money from the federal government in times of cash shortages to prevent panics.

In 1921, Edith Wharton became the first woman to win a Pulitzer Prize for literature, for *The Age of Innocence.*

Zane Grey wrote hundreds of popular westerns. He was born Pearl Gray, earned a dentistry degree from the University of Pennsylvania, and worked as a New York City dentist until 1904. *(Private Collection)*

AMERICAN WRITERS SEEK THEIR OWN VOICE

As the U.S. education system improved and literacy increased in the early 20th century, many Americans found themselves reading more. Several factors contributed to this trend. Many Americans had a greater awareness of improving society and themselves. Advances in technology made mass production printing much easier. Newspapers and magazines started putting ads in their publications, reducing the price to as low as a penny for a newspaper and five cents for a magazine. This decrease in production costs also meant there were many more magazines and books to choose from.

In literature, American tastes leaned toward romances and adventures. Romance authors who are now long forgotten had many titles selling more than a million copies, a number unheard of before the turn of the century. The two most popular adventure writers were Jack London who wrote the immensely popular *The Call of the Wild* (1903) and Zane Grey, who made the western novel popular with books like *Riders of the Purple Sage* (1912).

America had developed a strong writing tradition in the 19th century. Such writers as Herman Melville, Walt Whitman, and Nathaniel Hawthorne did establish the American voice that was lacking in music and art. American writers of the first two decades of the 20th century would strengthen that tradition, and their influence would start to spread worldwide. According to writer and critic Gertrude Stein, all of the literary change "since 1910 was due wholly to Americans."

Realism and social change were the themes of the best American writers of the era. Muckrakers such as Upton Sinclair brought about social change with works such as his book *The Jungle,* which exposed horrible conditions in the meat packing industry. Other realists, such as Frank Norris, were less political. Norris reacted against the more traditional, and popular, romance

SOCIALISTS AND THE WOBBLIES

As the gap between America's richest and poorest grew, many of its workers began to believe in socialism. Socialism is an economic system where government owns and runs most businesses, especially public services, such as railroads, utilities, etc. Socialists believe that when business is privately owned, as in America's capitalist system, workers are not treated fairly.

This was certainly true in the 1900s as many workers could not earn a decent wage, hours were long, and working conditions dangerous. Socialism grew in popularity during this decade and the Socialist leader, Eugene Debs, ran several times for president. He would get more than 400,000 votes in the 1908 election and more than 900,000 votes in the 1912 election.

In 1905, the most frustrated of the socialists formed the International Workers of the World, who became known as the Wobblies. The Wobblies believed in using direct action, like strikes, boycotts and even industrial sabotage to fight for workers' rights. Some Wobblies called for a general strike of all workers around the world, a strike to bring an end to capitalism.

The leader of the Wobblies was William Haywood, who had previously led the miners' union in the West. Not long after helping form the IWW, Haywood was put on trial for the murder of former Idaho governor Frank Steunenberg. Steunenberg had been a powerful opponent of unionizing Idaho's mineworkers. He was killed when his booby-trapped gate exploded in Caldwell, Idaho. Haywood was acquitted of the crime and continued to lead the IWW until its decline during the intensely patriotic atmosphere of World War I (1914–1918).

Theodore Dreiser's novel *Sister Carrie* was a failure when first published in 1900. His second, *Jennie Gerhardt*, did not come out until 1911. *(Private Collection)*

fiction and wrote about the daily, often tragic, lives of common men and women. He wanted to write "novels with a purpose," he said, and called his realism "the raw, naked thing that perplexes and fascinates." Norris's best known works are *McTeague* (1899) and *The Octopus* (1901). He died in 1902 at the age of 32.

Norris's successor in realism was Theodore Dreiser. Dreiser's *Sister Carrie*, published in 1900, took realism to another level as it dealt with all the harsh realities of urban life in the 20th century. Dreiser dealt with new themes such sexuality, consumerism, and suicide that shocked some readers. He also made some enemies by

"I simply want to tell about life as it is. Every human life is intensely interesting."

—Theodore Dreiser explaining his realist approach to writing

William Howard Taft won the 1908 election easily, but he had the tough job of succeeding Theodore Roosevelt as president. *(Smithsonian Institute)*

William Jennings Bryan had strong popular support outside of urban areas, but failed in all three attempts at the presidency. *(Library of Congress)*

blaming the new, greedy American society for his characters' problems, but nevertheless his work was popular. He greatly influenced future American writers including F. Scott Fitzgerald and Ernest Hemingway.

Another writer who was very popular during this era was Edith Wharton. As a woman, Wharton overcame tremendous obstacles to achieve success. She was not a realist writer, but wrote instead of the empty, selfish lives of the rich. Her works, such as *The House of Mirth* (1905) and *Ethan Frome* (1911) broke sales records and were widely acclaimed by fellow authors.

THE ELECTION OF 1908

Roosevelt admitted he made one big mistake during his presidency. After his election in 1904, he said he would not run again in 1908. There was no law against serving more than two terms, but there was a tradition, so Roosevelt decided his seven years as president would be enough. It was a promise he regretted very much as the 1908 election approached. He was extremely popular and would have been reelected easily, but he stuck to his word. Instead, he helped choose the Republican candidate he thought would carry on the policies he had begun. He chose his secretary of war, William Howard Taft.

In the election, Taft was opposed by Democrat William Jennings Bryan. It was the third time Bryan would run for the presidency and the third time he would lose. Taft won the popular vote by a little more than 1 million votes and the electoral vote 321 to 162. Roosevelt left the White House in 1909 to go on a long hunting trip to Africa and a tour of Europe. He was convinced he had left the country in good hands and was done with the presidency.

CHAPTER 4

THE TAFT PRESIDENCY, 1909–1912

WILLIAM HOWARD TAFT WAS BORN IN Cincinnati, Ohio, in 1857 to a distinguished political family. His father had a successful career serving as attorney general and secretary of war under President Ulysses S. Grant and as a minister to Austria and Russia. From the start, young William emulated his father and was trained to follow in his footsteps with a career in public service.

After Taft graduated Yale College in 1878 and Cincinnati Law School in 1880, he pursued a career as a judge. In 1887, when he was only 30, Taft was appointed to the Ohio Supreme Court. Two years later, President Benjamin Harrison appointed him solicitor

Henry Ford's Model T revolutionized the automobile industry, selling more than 15 million between 1908 and 1926. The mass-produced car revolutionized American life as well, changing where people lived and how they lived forever. *(Ford Motor Company)*

William Howard Taft was hand-picked by Theodore Roosevelt to carry on his square deal reform policies as president. *(Library of Congress)*

Woodrow Wilson was only the second Democrat elected U.S. president since Abraham Lincoln. The other was Grover Cleveland who was elected to two terms in 1884 and 1892.

general of the United States, but after just one year in Washington, Taft returned to Ohio as a circuit court judge and served for eight years.

The nation called on Taft again in 1900 when President McKinley asked him to serve on a commission trying to restore peace to the Philippines. Local rebels had been resisting U.S. occupation since the United States took over the island after the Spanish-American War. Taft would much rather have stayed a judge in Ohio, but his wife, Helen Herron Taft, and President McKinley persuaded him to accept the position.

Within a year, the Taft commission and the U.S. Army brought an end to the war in the Philippines, but not before approximately 4,000 Americans had died in battle. Taft was appointed governor of the islands and ruled very effectively for two years. He improved the court system and built schools, roads, and harbors. He purchased 400,000 acres from the Roman Catholic Church to give back to the Filipino people and promoted local self-government.

Taft's great success in the Philippines led President Roosevelt to appoint him secretary of war in 1903. Over the next five years, Taft became Roosevelt's most trusted aide. Roosevelt sent him to Panama in 1903 to help form its new government and to Cuba in 1906 to put down a revolt. Taft also took part in Roosevelt's Treaty of Portsmouth ending the Russo-Japanese War of 1904–05. Whenever Roosevelt traveled away from Washington, he left Taft in charge of running the government.

Twice during Roosevelt's presidency, he offered Taft his dream job—the opportunity to be a justice on the Supreme Court. Taft turned it down both times because his wife wanted him to be president. She knew her husband had a good chance to be the 1908 Republican candidate, and she was right. Roosevelt was at the peak of his popularity and power in 1908 and as the election drew near, he was able to pick his successor. He thought Taft an ideal choice because of his efficiency and his desire to continue Roosevelt's reform programs. Due to Roosevelt's immense popularity with the American people, Taft won the 1908 presidential election easily, defeating Democrat William Jennings Bryan.

DOMESTIC AFFAIRS AND ECONOMICS

Anyone who followed Teddy Roosevelt as president was going to be at a disadvantage. Roosevelt was not just loved by most of the American people, he was also a master politician. He knew how Washington worked and how to get what he wanted. He knew how to charm Congressmen and how to make deals. If those strategies did not work, he would just do what he wanted to do anyway. His energy matched that of the American people; at the start of a new century, both were ready to take on the world.

Taft freely admitted that he did not like politics and did not really want to be president. He had the

In 1910, Taft was the first president to throw out the first pitch of a baseball season. The tradition continues to this day.

With new machinery like this steam tractor ca. 1909, farmers could cultivate much more land than before and crop production for export increased. *(Library of Congress)*

In April and May 1910, Halley's Comet appeared brightly in the skies over the United States The comet posed no danger, but many people panicked. Some thought it was the end of the world, while others bought "comet pills" to protect them from the comet's poisonous gases.

THE BIRTH OF THE SCOUTS

Between 1900 and 1920, many children suffered under poverty and horrible working conditions, but there were people concerned with their welfare. In England, General Robert Baden-Powell observed during his military service that English boys had little experience in outdoor life or physical exercise. In 1907, he organized a camp for 20 boys and called his campers Boy Scouts. The following year, he published a manual called *Scouting for Boys* and the Boy Scout movement had begun. Baden-Powell taught the Boy Scouts camping skills, first aid, taking care of their health, and self-reliance. He also stressed the importance of loyalty, patriotism, and service to their community.

In 1909, American publisher William Boyce was visiting London when he got lost in a thick fog. An English Boy Scout helped Boyce find his way and would not accept a tip for his help. Boyce was so impressed that when he returned to the United States, he started the Boy Scouts of America. By 1919, there were more than 300,000 Boy Scouts.

In 1912, Daisy Low decided there should also be a Girl Scouts of America. To raise the money she needed to start the Girl Scouts, she sold her pearl necklace for $8,000 and opened the first camp in Savannah, Georgia. The Girl Scouts became a national organization in 1915. Today there are more than 7 million Boy Scouts and Girl Scouts in the United States.

Western farmers mainly supported the progressive wing of the Republican Party, which urged economic protection of American agriculture. *(National Archives)*

temperament of a judge—honest, but slow. He also did not believe in extending the powers of the presidency as Roosevelt had, so he would often wait for Congress to take the lead in governing. It was not the ideal temperament for a president in 1908, a fast-moving, reform-minded time. As a result, Taft's presidency would be marked by both accomplishments and failures. Taft said soon after his election that when someone said, "Mr. President," he looked around for Roosevelt. At times, Taft's biggest failure seemed to be simply that he was not Teddy Roosevelt.

In domestic affairs, Taft got in trouble right away with his tariff bill. A tariff is a tax on imported goods.

Those who favor a higher tariff believe it is good for American business because it drives out most foreign competition. However, the lack of competition means businesses can set their prices as high as they want and the American consumer pays higher prices. Those who favor a lower tariff believe the competition of foreign goods drives prices down and the American consumer benefits by paying lower prices for goods.

Even during Roosevelt's terms, the Republican Party had a strong division within it—the progressives and the conservatives, sometimes called the standpatters. The progressives were mostly westerners representing farming and small business interests. They favored social reforms and trust-busting to control big business. They also supported lower tariffs, which helped farmers export their goods. The conservatives were mostly easterners representing big business and industrial interests. They were against government intervention in business and favored very few social reforms. They also supported higher tariffs, which helped the more industrial businesses of the East.

Taft entered the White House with a reputation as a progressive and he originally submitted a low tariff bill to Congress. By the time it got through the House and Senate, however, it was a compromise. To get his bill passed, Taft made deals with conservative Republican leaders. He also agreed to abandon his support for a bill limiting the huge powers of the Speaker of the House, a bill progressives favored strongly. When Taft called the tariff bill "the best bill the Republican party ever passed," the progressives felt betrayed.

Taft also angered the conservationists within the progressive wing of the party. First, he hired his own secretary of the interior, Richard Ballinger, instead of keeping Roosevelt's man, James Garfield. When the head of the Forest Service, Gifford Pinchot, accused Ballinger of fraud and corruption in an Alaskan land deal, Taft fired Pinchot. The firing enraged Roosevelt

By 1910, there were 7 million telephones in the United States. *(AT&T)*

A method for collecting fingerprints at the scene of a crime was discovered in 1911. The first criminal convicted on fingerprint evidence was a burglar named Charlie Crispi.

New Mexico became a state in 1912. Above is the town plaza of Socorro in central New Mexico. *(Socorro Historical Society)*

and resulted in a severe split in the Republican party that would only worsen as Taft's term continued.

Despite the rift, Taft was able to get some things accomplished. He was a strong trustbuster, starting twice as many antitrust suits as Roosevelt had. In 1911, John Rockefeller's huge Standard Oil trust was dissolved. Taft also signed the Mann-Elkins Act, giving the Interstate Commerce Commission, rather than big business, control over the communications industry, including telephone, telegraph, and radio companies.

During Taft's term, Congress proposed two constitutional amendments, the first since 1870. The Sixteenth Amendment gave Congress the right to impose a national income tax and the Seventeenth Amendment provided for the direct election of U.S. senators. Prior to the amendment, senators were chosen by state legislatures. He also signed the Publicity Act, a law requiring political parties to reveal the sources of money spent in election campaigns. Both amendments were ratified as Taft was leaving office.

The expansion of the West continued during Taft's term, spurred on by the expanded Homestead Act of

"THE ONLY AMERICAN SAINT"

During the immigration wave of the late 19th and early 20th centuries, immigrants had little help from the government in adapting to American life. In the 1880s, private citizens started helping the immigrants by creating settlement houses where the immigrants could be fed, get medical care, and learn to read and write English. One of the earliest and most successful of the settlement houses was Hull-House in Chicago. It was founded by Jane Addams, a social reformer who was once described by a visitor to Hull House as "the only saint the United States has produced."

Addams was born into a well-to-do family in Cedarville, Illinois. Her father was a politician and a friend of Abraham Lincoln. Addams was born with a spinal defect that affected her activity as a child. She later had the problem corrected with surgery, but she said her experience with her handicap made her want to help others who were in need.

In 1889, she bought a run-down mansion in Chicago's west side slums and named it Hull-House after the building's ex-owner. After repairing the mansion, she offered local immigrants food, medical care, and English lessons. Addams also made Hull-House a place where immigrants could gather with their friends and take part in a concert or a play. Addams would hold German nights, Italian nights, and other ethnically focused nights, where immigrants could take pride in their heritage.

Addams became one of the leading social reformers of the 20th century and played a major role in the formation of the Progressive party in 1912. She worked for women's rights, child labor reforms, and world peace. In 1931, she received the Nobel Peace Prize, becoming the first American woman to win the prestigious award.

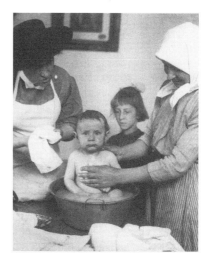

A visiting nurse from Hull-House teaches a mother how to bathe her baby. Few health services were available to the poor at the time. (*Library of Congress*)

In 1911, steel tycoon Andrew Carnegie donated $125 million to start the Carnegie Corporation, a charitable foundation. Over his lifetime, Carnegie donated more than $350 million to charity.

1909. The act increased the amount of land offered to homesteaders from 160 acres to 320 acres in sparsely populated areas of the West. Along with the continued development of western railroads and irrigation projects, new settlers flocked into the West. One result of this expansion of population was the admission of two new states to the union in 1912, Arizona and New Mexico.

Taft also had some success in passing several social reform bills. He established a Children's Bureau within the Department of Labor to help protect child laborers. He formed a Bureau of Mines to help protect

THE *TITANIC* SINKS!

On April 10, 1912, the British passenger ship *Titanic* began its maiden voyage from Southampton, England, to New York. It was the largest and most luxurious ship in the world and one of the marvels of modern technology. The *Titanic* was 882 feet long and had 16 separate watertight compartments that were supposed to make it unsinkable. Its confident captain, Edward Smith, hoped to break the speed record for the fastest crossing of the Atlantic Ocean.

On the night of April 14, a lookout spotted an iceberg dead ahead of the Titanic. The captain turned the ship to avoid it, but it was too late. The Titanic sideswiped the iceberg, causing damage to six of the compartments. Captain Smith knew the ship was going down and ordered the passengers into lifeboats. The problem was there were not nearly enough lifeboats for everyone onboard. Women and children were loaded on the lifeboats first, and they watched as the *Titanic* sank, taking 1,517 lives with it. Several American millionaires were among the

A 1912 artist's version of the sinking of the *Titanic.* The ship actually split in two just before sinking. *(New York Times)*

dead including John Jacob Astor and Isidor Straus, department store founder, and his wife Ida. The Strauses' fate became quite famous at the time. Ida was pushed onto a lifeboat of women and children, but she declined, preferring to stay with her husband, saying, according to the May 13, 1912, *New York Times,* "We have been together a long time. I will not leave you. Where you go, I shall go."

There were two main factors in the sinking of the *Titanic.* The ship was traveling too fast for an area where icebergs were known to be present. Also, the ship's steel and rivets were weakened by the frigid waters of the North Atlantic. The sinking of the *Titanic* led to new safety regulations. Ships would now be required to carry enough lifeboats for all onboard and maintain 24-hour radio watches. The night the *Titanic* sunk, another ship, the *Californian,* was less than 20 miles away but had no radio operator to hear the *Titanic's* calls for help.

One of the *Titanic's* lifeboats carries survivors to safety the following morning. More than 1,500 passengers died in the tragedy. *(Library of Congress)*

the health and safety of mine workers and he signed a bill providing for compensation for injured workers. Despite these reforms and a strong economy, the progressives were not impressed. Halfway through Taft's term, they were already looking for a new leader and candidate for the 1912 election.

FOREIGN POLICY: DOLLAR DIPLOMACY

Like Roosevelt, Taft was an imperialist. He felt the United States needed to expand its influence abroad, but in his words he wanted to substitute "dollars for bullets." His plan was to increase influence over foreign governments by convincing American businessmen to invest abroad. If there was any resistance to these investments, he believed in using diplomatic pressure rather than military threat. This approach to foreign policy became known as dollar diplomacy and had only limited success.

One success was in China, where Taft and his secretary of state Philander Knox convinced several American bankers to help finance railroad construction. However, Taft wanted to expand the American investments into Manchuria, an area of China that Japan and Russia had fought to acquire for many years. Taft thought building a Chinese railroad there would decrease Japanese and Russian influence in the area. The plan backfired when Japan and Russia protested, and Taft withdrew rather than risk a military confrontation. Taft concentrated his dollar diplomacy in Latin America because of the importance of the Panama Canal. He not only promoted investments in the area, but he also tried to put Americans in charge of Latin American businesses whenever he could. Again his plans backfired. In 1909 the leader of Nicaragua, Jose Zelaya, resisted American influence. The Taft administration sent marines to the country to support a revolt to overthrow Zelaya, and a new government

The National Urban League was founded in New York City in 1910 to assist southern blacks moving north to find jobs. Between 1910 and 1920, 300,000 African Americans moved north in a movement known as the Great Migration.

William Taft and John Kennedy are the only presidents buried at Arlington National Cemetery.

THE QUEST FOR THE POLES

In the early 1900s, a race was on among explorers to be the first to reach the North and South Poles. The American explorer in the North Pole race was Robert Peary. Peary had dreamed of reaching the North Pole for 20 years and had made several attempts—all failures. In July 1908, he set off from New York aboard his ship, the *Roosevelt*, on another expedition. On hand to see him off was President Teddy Roosevelt, a staunch supporter of polar exploration.

After wintering on Ellesmere Island, Canada, Peary took off for the Pole in February 1909. Along with him, he had six American assistants, including Matthew Henson, an African American who had accompanied Peary on all the previous Pole attempts, and 17 Inuit. The expedition's 100 dogs pulled 19 sledges carrying six tons of supplies. On April 7, 1909, Peary took off from his final camp, accompanied by Henson and several Inuit, for the last leg of the journey. When they reached the area of the North Pole, Peary took measurements of the sun to verify his location and raised several flags, including the U.S. stars and stripes.

Peary returned to the United States a hero and was made a rear admiral in the Navy in 1911. From the beginning, there has been controversy surrounding Peary's claim to have reached the North Pole. Some geographers doubt his measurements were correct, due to bad weather and visibility on the day he reached the Pole. However, most experts agree that he was at least close enough to the Pole to claim its discovery. (Due in large part to racism, Henson did not receive recognition for his achievement until 1944, when he was awarded a Congressional medal.)

Two years after Peary reached the North Pole, a Norwegian explorer, Roald Amundsen, became the first man to reach the South Pole. The world's two last unexplored regions had been conquered.

Early 1900s polar explorers did not have the benefit of modern equipment such as snowmobiles and waterproof nylon. They achieved their amazing exploits wearing fur and skin coats and using dogsleds. *(Library of Congress)*

led many in Latin America and the United States to view Taft's dollar diplomacy as simply exploitation.

Toward the end of his term, Taft tried to save his foreign policy record by negotiating trade agreements with Canada, France, and Great Britain to lower tariffs. By this time, however, Taft's lack of strong leadership had weakened his presidency. The agreement he reached with Canada was rejected by Canadian voters, and his agreements with France and Great Britain were rejected by the Senate.

In one critical area of foreign policy, Taft chose to remain uninvolved. During his term, Europe seemed on the edge of disaster. For many years, France, England, and Germany had competed for colonies and world influence. This conflict led to two major alliances. Germany joined with Austria-Hungary and Italy in the Triple Alliance. France and England joined with Russia in the Triple Entente. As each side built up their military strength, war seemed unavoidable. Taft managed to keep the United States a world power during these critical years, but exactly where it stood was still unclear. As it turned out, it had very little time left to decide.

Many families needed the income from their children's labor to survive. Above is a young female textile worker. *(Library of Congress)*

LABOR STRIFE

Progress in workers' rights continued to be slow during Taft's administration. Trusts were busted, but many workers still worked 12-hour days in unsafe conditions for low wages. As labor and management fought angrily over these rights, strikes became more common and

"I'm tired of listening to all this babble for reform. America is a h—— of a success."

—Speaker of the House Joseph Cannon disparaging the progressive movement of the early 1900s

Labor and management clashed frequently in the early 1900s. Some workers, like those on the right, thought communism was a better economic system. Many Americans feared immigrants and communists, often equating the two groups as troublemakers. *(Library of Congress)*

"I can hire half the working class to kill the other half."

—Railroad tycoon Jay Gould describing the struggle between labor and management

more violent. Sometimes strikers would burn or bomb factories and attack workers who crossed their picket lines. Management hired guards and strikebreakers to combat the strikers. Their battles resulted in many deaths, usually among the striking workers.

In 1911, a terrible tragedy helped publicize the plight of many workers. On March 25, a fire broke out at the Triangle Shirtwaist Company, a sweatshop in New York City. (A sweatshop is a factory where people work under unsafe conditions for very low wages.) Most of the employees were immigrant women, many under the age of 16. As they tried to escape the fire, they found the stairway exit doors locked to prevent stealing. The building's single fire escape collapsed as workers tried to flee.

By the time the fire was under control, 100 women had burned to death and another 46 died jumping from the ninth floor windows. The building had recently passed a fire inspection by city inspectors. The public outrage over this incident resulted in several New York labor laws concerning workplace safety, employment of women and children, limits on working hours, and workers' compensation.

One of the most important strikes of the decade took place in January and February 1912 at the textile mills in Lawrence, Massachusetts. The state had just passed a law reducing the workweek limit from 56 hours to 54, and in response mill owners cut wages 3½ percent, down to $6 a week. Led by one of their unions, the IWW (Industrial Workers of the World), the 23,000 textile workers, including many women and children, went on strike.

Sympathetic workers across New England joined the walkout until the number reached more than 250,000 strikers. The strike dragged on for six weeks as management refused to negotiate with the workers. The state's National Guard and private police were called in to keep the peace, but several strikers were killed in clashes between the two sides. When police assaulted a group of women and children, public outrage forced the mill owners to concede. The IWW negotiated higher wages and reduced working hours for the textile workers.

Labor Day was proclaimed a national holiday in 1894. Above, workers march in the New York City Labor Day parade ca. 1909. *(Library of Congress)*

"I'm glad to be going. This is the lonesomest place in the world."

—President Taft upon leaving the White House in 1913

Woodrow Wilson spent most of his life as a teacher and university president before winning the 1912 presidential election. *(Library of Congress)*

During the campaign of 1912, there was an assassination attempt on Teddy Roosevelt in Milwaukee, Wisconsin. The assassin's bullet was slowed down by the manuscript of Roosevelt's speech, and he suffered only a broken rib. Despite the injury, Roosevelt insisted on finishing his speech before getting medical attention.

The abuses of child labor continued to be a problem during Taft's administration. Several states passed laws limiting the number of child workers and working hours, but progress was very slow. In 1908, the NCLC (National Child Labor Committee) hired photographer Lewis Hine to take photos showing the horrible conditions for working children. Hine often had to disguise himself as an inspector or salesman to get his photos as factory owners tried to hide the truth. As Hine's photos of children in coal mines, sweatshops, and textile mills appeared in newspapers and magazines, more of the American public became involved in child labor reform.

As the battle between labor and management grew more violent, Taft established the Commission on Industrial Relations to investigate the problem. Their 1912 report clearly favored labor as they concluded that workers had not received a fair share of the wealth created by their own labor. The report also said that about one-third of America's workers were living in "abject poverty" and that the battle between labor and management was "practically a civil war." The commission had no power to enact changes, but the report did publicize the problems further.

THE ELECTION OF 1912

As the election of 1912 approached, President Taft was in trouble. He had not been able to prevent the split within his Republican party between the progressives and conservatives. Progressives had wanted to nominate Senator Robert La Follette of Wisconsin at the Republican convention, but La Follette's health was failing at the time. They turned instead to former president Teddy Roosevelt. Roosevelt had always regretted declining to run in 1908, and he was very disappointed in Taft's performance.

The campaign between Taft and Roosevelt for the Republican nomination was hard fought. At one point, Roosevelt called Taft a "fathead" and Taft called

President Taft at first refused statehood to Arizona because its constitution allowed the recall of judges. Arizona removed the law from its constitution, and Taft agreed to grant it statehood. Right after becoming a state, Arizona's legislature put the recall law back in its constitution.

ADMISSION TO THE UNION

Three states were added to the Union between 1900 and 1920—Oklahoma, Arizona, and New Mexico. These additions brought the total number of states to 48. In 1959 the addition of far-flung Alaska and Hawaii brought the total to the present number of 50. The question of adding new states was anticipated by the founding fathers in the Constitution in which they gave Congress the power to increase the number of states. The Constitution also gave the president a role in the process since he can always veto any act of Congress.

In 1803, President Thomas Jefferson signed the Enabling Act establishing the procedures for territories to become states. The act required the people of a territory to hold a convention and create a state constitution. The act gave Congress the power to accept, reject, or amend the state constitution before admitting the territory into the Union.

Even with the procedures made clear by these laws, the road to statehood has not always been easy. This was especially true in the years before the Civil War as Congress was bitterly divided over whether new states should be allowed to sanction slavery. The debate led to a series of compromises starting with the Missouri Compromise of 1820 when Missouri was admitted as a slave state and a line was drawn on its southern border as the boundary between free and slave territory. The compromises were designed to avoid civil war, but they only delayed it until 1861.

Utah first applied for statehood in 1849, but it was denied because of the state's law allowing polygamy, or marrying more than one person. Many Mormons lived in Utah and they considered polygamy as an important part of their religion. The Mormon Church finally rejected the practice of polygamy in the 1890s, and Utah was admitted to the Union in 1896.

"My hat's in the ring! The fight is on and I'm stripped to the buff."

—Teddy Roosevelt announcing his candidacy for the presidency in 1912

William Taft weighed more than 300 pounds, making him by far the largest president ever. He once got stuck in the White House bathtub and had to be pulled out by several of his staff members.

Roosevelt a "demagogue." Roosevelt won most of the state primaries, but Taft and his conservative supporters controlled the convention. They refused to allow some of Roosevelt's delegates to be counted, and Taft won the nomination.

Roosevelt and the progressives were so furious they stormed out of the convention and formed a third party. It was originally called the Progressive party, but it came to be known as the Bull Moose party after Roosevelt said he "felt as strong as a bull moose" for the campaign. He named his program the New Nationalism and called for 8-hour days for workers, child labor reforms, voting rights for all Americans, and more regulation of big business.

The Democrats nominated Woodrow Wilson, the governor of New Jersey. Wilson was known as a strong progressive and ran on a program called the New Freedom. He believed in limits on the size of corporations, lower tariffs, and government regulation of the U.S. banking system. He believed in a strong federal government and promised fair treatment for labor and African Americans.

Roosevelt made the strongest showing any third party candidate ever had, but it was not enough. With Roosevelt and Taft splitting the Republican voters, Wilson won easily. The popular vote was fairly close: Wilson had 6.3 million votes, Roosevelt 4.1 million, and Taft 3.5 million. (American voters showed how eager they were for real reform by casting nearly 1 million votes for the Socialist candidate, Eugene Debs.) The electoral vote, however, was not close: Wilson had 435 electoral votes, Roosevelt 88, and Taft only 8. The United States was ready for its New Freedom.

CHAPTER 5

THE PROGRESSIVE ERA AND WOODROW WILSON, 1913–1916

WOODROW WILSON'S FAMILY BIBLE states that he was born "Thomas Woodrow Wilson on December 28, 1856, at 12¾ o'clock at night." He was never sure what time that meant so he celebrated his birthday on December 28. Other aspects of his childhood are clearer, and three would prove to have a big effect on his development.

First, he seemed to be a very slow student and still could not read at the age of ten. It is now believed he had a learning disability called dyslexia, a handicap

Spectators jam the steps of the U.S. Capitol in Washington, D.C., for the inauguration of Woodrow Wilson in 1913. *(Library of Congress)*

Wilson served as president of Princeton University from 1902 to 1910, where he reformed academics and modernized the university teaching system.
(*Princeton University Library*)

President Wilson's first wife, Ellen Axson, died in 1914, 18 months after Wilson took office. He married Edith Galt in 1915.

not understood at the time. His father, a Presbyterian minister, took over his son's education and taught him through speaking and writing. These talents would be keys to Wilson's success later in life as a professor and politician. Second, his father's deep religious feelings also influenced Wilson throughout his life. Woodrow developed a strong sense of righteousness, a belief that one knows what is right and wrong, and a resistance to compromise on one's belief. Finally, Wilson was born in Staunton, Virginia, and grew up throughout the South during the hard Reconstruction years after the Civil War. He saw the consequences of war, and the suffering it caused innocent people.

Wilson knew from a young age that his interest was government and public office. He graduated from Princeton University in 1879 and Virginia Law School in 1881 with the intention of entering politics from his law practice. However, he discovered he had little talent as a lawyer and decided to become a college professor of law and government. He received his Ph.D. in politics from Johns Hopkins University in 1885 and wrote a very successful book, *Congressional Government.*

Wilson's teaching career flourished, and he gave credit for his success to the oratorical and writing skills he received from his father as a child. In 1890, he became a professor of law and economics at his alma mater, Princeton University in New Jersey. During the 1890s, Wilson's skills as a teacher and a proponent of government reform made him a nationally known public figure. In 1902, he was named president of Princeton and spent the next ten years turning the university into one of the great schools in the country. His views on educational and social reform made him so admired nationally that many political leaders began to consider him for political office.

In 1910, the Democratic party bosses in New Jersey persuaded him to run for governor. The state government was one of the most corrupt in the United States,

Machinery was changing the face of farming in the early 20th century, but many poorer farmers still used old-fashioned methods. Spreading prosperity made such scenes increasingly rare. *(International Harvester)*

and the bosses thought Wilson's inexperience would make him easy to control. Wilson won the election easily and shocked the bosses by taking total control of the government. In just two years, he forced passage of several reform bills, turning New Jersey into one of the most progressive states in the nation. His new laws established direct primary elections and brought the railroads and public utilities under state control. He also signed an anti-corruption act and several school reform laws.

At the Democratic national convention in June 1912, party leaders knew that whomever they nominated to be their presidential candidate would win the election. The Republicans were sharply divided between Taft and Roosevelt and the country was ready for a change. Progressives were at the height of their popularity, and the Democrats knew that the progressive Roosevelt was their strongest opponent. It took the convention 46 ballots to choose a candidate, but when party leader William Jennings Bryan threw his support to Wilson, the nomination was his.

Wilson would be elected president in both 1912 and 1916, and his two terms saw huge changes in the United States. The Wilson years would complete the transition that had started years before, from the old

"We have been proud of our industrial achievements, but we have not stopped thoughtfully enough to count the human cost."

—Woodrow Wilson speaking on the rights of the people

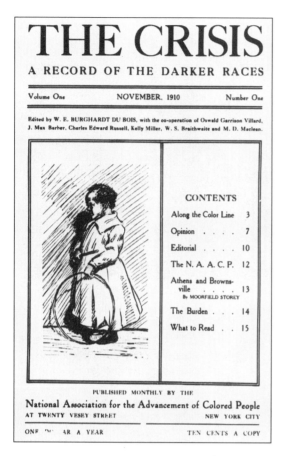

THE CRISIS

A RECORD OF THE DARKER RACES

Volume One   NOVEMBER, 1910   Number One

Edited by W. E. BURGHARDT DU BOIS, with the co-operation of Oswald Garrison Villard, J. Max Barber, Charles Edward Russell, Kelly Miller, W. S. Braithwaite and M. D. Maclean.

CONTENTS

Along the Color Line   3

Opinion   7

Editorial   10

The N. A. A. C. P.   12

Athens and Browns-
ville   13
By MOORFIELD STOREY

The Burden   14

What to Read . . .   15

PUBLISHED MONTHLY BY THE

National Association for the Advancement of Colored People
AT TWENTY VESEY STREET   NEW YORK CITY

ONE DOLLAR A YEAR   TEN CENTS A COPY

The first issue of *The Crisis*, shown above, appeared in 1910. It was the official NAACP publication. *(Crisis Publishing Co., Inc.)*

In 1916, President Wilson appointed Louis Brandeis to the Supreme Court, the first Jew to serve on the court.

rural United States to the modern technological country it is today. In foreign affairs, the United States would take part in a war to make the world "safe for democracy," as Wilson later put it. On the home front, Wilson's leadership would bring about sweeping government and social reforms.

A REMARKABLE PERIOD OF REFORMS

When Wilson was elected president in 1912, the country also elected many other progressive Democrats to Congress. For the first two years of his term, Wilson would have strong support of all bills submitted to the House and Senate. The result was a remarkable string of new reform laws bringing about tremendous government and social change. Wilson said his primary task was to rid the country of "special privileges" and he began with the tariff.

Wilson believed that the high rates of Taft's 1909 tariff bill hurt the American consumer. Like other progressives, he believed high tariffs on foreign goods forced consumers to buy American-made products. Without foreign competition, American businesses could set prices as they wanted and create monopolies. In October 1913, Wilson signed the Underwood Tariff Act, which drastically cut tariffs. On certain goods such as food, wool, steel, and iron, which the United States produced very cheaply, tariffs were eliminated. U.S. companies would now have to compete with foreign companies, so prices for consumers would fall.

Another important aspect of the Underwood Act was the first use of the personal income tax made legal by the Sixteenth Amendment ratified earlier in 1913. High tariffs had been a source of income to run the federal government, so the income tax was needed to keep the

MORE THAN READING, WRITING AND ARITHMETIC

A big issue for progressives during the 1910s was education. They wanted not only to get children out of the work force but also to put them into quality schools. The amount of money spent on education doubled during the decade, from less than $500 million to more than $1 billion, and the number of teachers increased by more than 150,000. Many states passed compulsory education laws. The one-room schoolhouse was rapidly disappearing throughout the country as more high schools and kindergartens came into operation. As the number of immigrant students increased, many educators felt it was important that schools teach children how to contribute to American society.

Two educators rose to particular prominence during the 1910s. In 1912, Maria Montessori published her ideas on early education in *The Montessori Method.* She believed that education of the young should be geared toward their interests. She felt this freedom would make children want to learn and make them easier to teach throughout the rest of their educa-

Many Americans wanted immigrant children to be thoroughly Americanized. The above poster offers English lessons in six languages.
(Library of Congress)

tion. Montessori preschools became popular in the United States during the 1910s, and the teaching method proved very successful. A Montessori student usually could read and write before the age of five and often preferred schoolwork to play. Montessori schools continue to be popular today.

In 1916, John Dewey published his theory of education in *Democracy and Education.* Dewey opposed rote-learning, or memorization, as the primary method of teaching. He favored instead varied activities, such as experiments and field trips, that would teach problem-solving rather than just facts. He believed in schools being small "societies" with interaction among students and teachers trained in the most modern methods. Dewey felt this social approach to education would better prepare students for life in a democratic society. Dewey and Montessori would have a huge influence on 20th century education as the emphasis switched from the school to the student.

---

government running. The first tax was small and only affected corporations and higher-income Americans, but it would grow steadily over the years until the present day, when it is a major source of government income.

Wilson's next target was the U.S. banking system, which he felt was under the control of a small group of bankers and financiers. The financial panic of 1907 convinced Wilson that the federal government should have power over the country's banks. In 1913, Congress passed

W. E. B. DuBois believed African Americans would not be granted their civil rights until they demanded them. He spent his career in the civil rights movement. *(Library of Congress)*

THE INVISIBLE EMPIRE

The Ku Klux Klan, or KKK, was founded in 1865 in Tennessee by six former Confederate army officers. Its purpose was to overthrow the Reconstruction state governments that had been put into power after the Civil War in the former Confederate states. The Klan looked upon these governments as oppressive and opposed efforts to give blacks the vote and include them in white society. The Klan grew increasingly violent until 1871 when Congress passed the Force Bill to enforce the Fourteenth Amendment of the Constitution, which guaranteed the rights of all citizens. Hundreds of Klansmen were arrested, and the organization temporarily faded from prominence.

By 1915, black leaders such as W. E. B. DuBois were calling for civil rights, including voting and anti-lynching laws, for African Americans. One reaction in the South was the revival of the KKK, after Georgia granted the organization a state charter. The new Klan adopted many of the habits of the original group. Its members wore white robes and hoods and burned crosses to frighten KKK targets. The Klan's main target was still blacks, but it now attacked any outside influence it believed threatened American ideals, and its victims included Roman Catholics, Jews, and union organizers.

The Klan's terrorism grew, especially in the South where local officials often supported the group. The Klan's tactics included demonstrations where their enemies might be warned to leave town. Their activities usually escalated to include beatings and murders especially of African Americans, many of whom were lynched without trial or even cause. By the end of the decade, the Klan had grown to about 100,000 members, and their brutal crimes were a leading cause for the black migration north between 1910 and 1920.

In 1916, Jeannette Rankin from Montana became the first woman to be elected to the U.S. House of Representatives.

The Ku Klux Klan violently opposed the integration of blacks into American society. Its symbol of terror was a burning cross. This photo is from *Birth of a Nation,* a film that included a dramatization of the Klan's activities. *(Private Collection)*

his Federal Reserve System bill, completely restructuring U.S. banking. The bill created one central Federal Reserve Bank and 12 regional banks, all under the control of the Federal Reserve Board. The board had the power to regulate credit and the nation's money supply. The board would set interest rates, buy and sell government bonds, and issue paper currency backed by gold reserves.

In 1914, Wilson also created the Federal Trade Commission to fight the abuses of big business. The commission had the authority to review business mergers to prevent the formation of trusts. Wilson also signed a stronger antitrust bill, the Clayton Antitrust Act, which made unfair business practices such as price discrimination illegal. One of the most important aspects of this act gave unions the right to strike, boycott, and picket.

In the last year of his first term, Wilson won Congress's approval of several other progressive measures. He increased federal aid for schools and highway construction. He secured an eight-hour workday for railroad workers and unemployment compensation

"No one but the president seems to be expected to look out for the general interests of the country."

—President Wilson
on the powers of
the presidency in 1913

ANOTHER WOMEN'S CAMPAIGN: BIRTH CONTROL

In 1873, the U.S. government passed the Comstock Law, making it a crime for anyone to distribute information about birth control, even doctors and nurses. At the time, such material was considered obscene, but as the population grew and attitudes became more liberal, many started to consider such information a right. While many women fought for the right to vote in the early 20th century, one woman almost single-handedly led the birth control movement.

Margaret Sanger was born in Corning, New York, in 1879, the sixth of 11 children. Sanger became a nurse in 1912 and worked with the poor of New York City. In her work, she saw many women become ill and die from constant pregnancies. She became convinced that access to birth control information was the key to both improved health for women and the freedom to control their own lives.

In 1914, Sanger started to distribute a newspaper called *The Woman Rebel.* It contained birth control information and attacks on the Comstock Law. She was charged with issuing obscene material and only escaped prison by fleeing to Europe. Sanger returned to America in 1916 when the charges against her were dropped and opened the nation's first birth control clinic in Brooklyn, New York. She was arrested and served a 30-day jail sentence for "maintaining a public nuisance."

After her release, Sanger won a court case that gave doctors the right to distribute birth control information. She continued to fight the Comstock Law until it was finally overturned in 1936. In 1917, Sanger formed the National Birth Control League to organize the national fight for birth control. This organization would later become Planned Parenthood, which today continues the fight for women's birth control rights.

"The bill is to have the government do for children what it has already done for calves and pigs."

—Senator William Borah of Idaho on submitting a child labor bill to Congress in 1916

In 1913, America's first gas station opened in Pittsburgh, Pennsylvania. It sold 30 gallons of gas the first day.

"Every time I lower the price a dollar, we gain a thousand new buyers."

—Henry Ford on why he kept lowering the price of his Model T car

for federal workers. He signed two bills for farmers helping them receive credit and obtain loans. He even managed to get a federal child labor law passed that limited the employment of children under 14. However, this victory would only be temporary, because the U.S. Supreme Court overturned the law in 1918 as unconstitutional. It would be another 20 years before a strong federal child labor law would finally be passed.

One issue of Wilson's New Freedom program failed—civil rights for African Americans. Despite his election promises to help blacks, Wilson did nothing. It is not certain why Wilson did not follow through on his promise. It is thought he might have made deals with southern congressional leaders to get his other New Freedom bills passed. He also had many southerners on his staff and one, Postmaster General Albert Burleson, even convinced Wilson to segregate black and white federal workers. When asked about his support of segregation, Wilson simply said he believed it was in the best interests of African Americans and protected them from "friction and criticism."

HENRY FORD REVOLUTIONIZES MODERN INDUSTRY

Henry Ford had introduced his Model T automobile in 1908 to mediocre sales, but he had an idea about increasing efficiency—and profits—through improvements in assembly line production. By 1914, Ford's assembly line efficiency would revolutionize U.S. industry. Giving each worker a particular duty to perform, Ford cut the time it took to assemble a Model T from 13 hours to an hour and a half. He produced 250,000 cars in 1914 and 500,000 in 1915.

Ford also doubled his workers' salary from $2.50 a day to $5 and reduced their workday to eight hours. This not only made his workers content, it also made them customers—they could now afford to buy a

Model T. He then initiated a profit-sharing program for his workers to encourage productivity even more. To cut costs, Ford began producing his own parts, including glass and steel. With all these savings in production costs, Ford was able to drop the cost of a Model T from $825 in 1908 to $360 in 1916, a price within the reach of the average American family.

Ford's company profits in 1916 were $60 million, and his mass production system would be copied around the country. More important, however, Ford almost single-handedly turned the United States into a consumer economy by offering higher pay and cheaper goods. It was also the first step in making the United States a mobile society—with cars, Americans could go anywhere, anytime. It was a development that would effect the entire century.

LONG DISTANCE CALLS: THE WORLD SHRINKS

In 1876, Alexander Graham Bell uttered the famous words, "Watson, come here, I want you," and the telephone was born. In 1915, Bell made another call to Watson and said the same words, but this time, he was in San Francisco and Watson was in New York. It was the first transcontinental long distance telephone call and it traveled over 3,400 miles of copper wire and 130,000 telephone poles.

The next communication technology was wireless transmission. Guglielmo Marconi had invented the wireless telegraph in 1894, and it had been used mainly to send Morse code signals at sea. The *Titanic* sent Morse code distress signals in the hours before its sinking, and other ships were able to rescue some of its survivors. American scientists and inventors made advances in technology, especially in tubes and receivers, until the transmission of the human voice over great distances, called radio, became possible. In 1915, U.S. Navy personnel spoke to each other between Washington, D.C., and the Panama Canal. Later that year, the navy made a broadcast from Washington, D.C., to Hawaii.

By 1920, stations in Detroit and Pittsburgh began regular broadcasting of music and news to listeners at home with radio receivers. A new era in American entertainment had begun.

The first taxi cabs appeared in New York and Chicago in 1915. At first, they were called jitneys because a ride in one cost a jitney, slang for a nickel.

The transcontinental telephone line reached the Nevada-Utah border in 1914. It would be complete by the following year. (*Smithsonian Institute*)

Mexican revolutionary Pancho Villa killed many Americans in raids on border towns in 1916. Wilson told General Pershing "Capture Villa, dead or alive." *(Library of Congress)*

> *"What this country needs is a good five-cent cigar."*
>
> —Vice President Thomas Marshall during a long Senate debate in 1915

MORAL DIPLOMACY IN LATIN AMERICA

Wilson and Roosevelt had very similar domestic policies. They fought very hard for many progressive reforms, but they did differ on foreign policy. Just as Taft wanted to replace Roosevelt's bullets with dollars in foreign policy, Wilson wanted to replace Taft dollars with morals. He felt it was America's duty to teach other nations how to become democracies. In 1916, Wilson signed the Jones Bill, granting the Philippines much more self-rule, but in Latin America, moral diplomacy was sometimes not enough.

Wilson showed his desire to improve Latin American relations with a $20 million reparation payment to Colombia for the role the United States had played in the Panamanian revolt under Roosevelt. His efforts in other Latin American nations, however, again often relied on bullets. In Nicaragua, Wilson allowed U.S. troops to remain and negotiated a treaty with the Nicaraguan government that forbade any other nation from building a canal in the country. The United States paid $3 million to Nicaragua, but the nation could have made far more by building a second canal connecting the Atlantic and Pacific Oceans. Wilson also sent U.S. troops to Haiti and the Dominican Republic after revolts there threatened U.S. interests.

It was in Mexico, however, that Wilson's Latin American diplomacy would have its strongest test. In 1913, the elected government of Mexico was overthrown by the dictator Victoriano Huerta. Wilson refused to recognize the new leader and actively supported a revolt by Huerta's opponent Venustiano Carranza.

Relations between the two countries remained strained until the next year when fourteen U.S. sailors were illegally arrested by Mexican officials in Tampico. They were soon released, but Wilson was furious and ordered a blockade of the Mexican port of Veracruz in retaliation. A second reason for the blockade was the approach of a German ship carrying ammunition for Huerta's troops. When U.S. troops landed at Veracruz, a battle broke out resulting in the deaths of 126 Mexicans and 19 Americans. War was avoided only when Argentina, Brazil, and Chile mediated a peace and installed Carranza as Mexico's new leader.

In 1916, the situation again flared up when Carranza's rival, Pancho Villa, killed 16 Americans aboard a train in northern Mexico. Villa was trying to get the United States to intervene in Mexico and weaken Carranza. When Wilson did nothing, Villa raided U.S. towns over the border in New Mexico and Texas killing scores of Americans. Wilson finally sent 6,000 troops led by General John Pershing over the border with orders to "capture Villa, dead or alive."

The last surviving passenger pigeon died in the Cincinnati Zoo in 1914. A hundred years before, there were millions of passenger pigeons, but the species was hunted into extinction.

Louis Armstrong's innovative trumpet playing helped popularize New Orleans jazz among both white and black audiences. *(Library of Congress)*

The term *ragtime* came from an early description of the music's beat as ragged.

For nearly a year, Pershing chased Villa without success. The mission was also a diplomatic failure as Carranza and the Mexican people considered the U.S. troops' presence as an invasion. In early 1917, Wilson called Pershing and his troops back to the United States. They were needed for a far bigger battle as the United States was being drawn into the Great War in Europe.

FIRST AMERICAN MUSIC: RAGTIME AND JAZZ

In the early 20th century, a blend of several African-American music styles would create the first uniquely American music: ragtime and jazz. Ragtime had its origins in the 1880s as an African-American musical form emphasizing beat and melody. It became especially popular during the 1900s with the rags of Scott Joplin whose "Maple Leaf Rag" was the most popular ragtime song of the decade. Another African-American form of music, blues, also started gaining popularity in the 1900s. Blues had its roots in rural black America and was a mix of plantation songs and spirituals. "Jelly Roll" Morton published "New Orleans Blues" in 1902, but the first popular blues song was W. C. Handy's "St. Louis Blues" in 1912.

In the 1910s, black musicians in New Orleans created jazz by combining elements of ragtime and blues and adding an urban feel. Ragtime and blues declined in popularity as jazz became America's music. Black soldiers took the music to Europe during World War I, and white musicians joined African Americans in creating the first American form of music with worldwide popularity. It became so popular by the 1920s that the decade is often called the Jazz Age. The early innovators of jazz included "Jelly Roll" Morton, Joe Oliver, and Louis Armstrong.

A very important aspect of these musical developments in the early 20th century is that it was the first time black Americans could start to feel a national pride that they were contributing something important to American society. There was still much racism involved in the industry, and black musicians were often cheated by white producers. While white recordings of ragtime and jazz outsold black recordings, the innovations of ragtime and blues were a significant step forward for black American pride.

THE ARMORY SHOW

Throughout the first two decades of the 20th century, American artists tried to find a uniquely American style of art. At the end of the 19th century, the best American artists, such as Mary Cassatt, James Whistler, and John Singer Sargent followed European styles and even lived in Europe. In 1908, a group of American artists tried to break from European influence and formed the Ashcan school.

Ashcan artists, such as Robert Henri and George Bellows, believed in realism and found art in urban settings, even the ashcans on the dirty streets. The style was closely connected to the progressive movement of the decade as reformers sought social changes, particularly in poor urban areas. Bellows became the most famous of the Ashcan artists as his work seemed to catch both progressive ideals and Roosevelt's idea of the strenuous life. His paintings of boxers were especially popular with their energetic, stripped-down look at life.

Ashcan artists held a show in 1910 that was so controversial riot police had to be called out to control the crowd. However, it was not until the famous Armory show in New York in 1913 that this American style found its true place in world art. The Armory show was the most important art exhibit of its time. It presented more than 300 artists, about 100 of whom were American, and more than 1,300 paintings. The show traveled on to Chicago and Boston and more than 300,000 Americans attended.

"It looks like an explosion in a shingle factory."

—An art critic's opinion of Marcel Duchamp's painting, *Nude Descending a Staircase,* at the Armory Exhibit in New York City in 1913

In 1913, the tango dance craze swept the nation. The dance was banned in Boston and other cities because it required dancers to hold each other too closely.

In 1913, Cracker Jack started putting a small toy in every box of its peanut-and-popcorn snack. The inventor of the snack was F. W. Rueckman, and the little boy on the box's label was his grandson, who died of pneumonia at the age of eight.

The Armory show was an eye-opening education for the American public but a big disappointment for its artists. The new, daring works by Europeans such as Pablo Picasso, Henri Matisse, and Marcel Duchamp made even Ashcan artists look out-of-date and unimaginative. New nonrealistic styles such as cubism and expressionism were taking over the art world. Realism, even a fresh American realism, seemed old and dull in comparison. American artists would have to wait for their voice to be heard.

CHAPTER 6

WORLD WAR I ERUPTS, 1914–1918

T HE GREAT WAR OF EUROPE CAME TO be known as World War I only after World War II in the 1940s. Its strongest roots go back to the two alliances that were formed after the Franco-Prussian War of 1870–71. After France suffered a humiliating loss to Germany in that war, both countries formed military pacts with their allies for more security. In 1882, Germany, Austria-Hungary, and Italy formed the Triple Alliance. By 1905, France formed the Triple Entente with Russia and England. Each side competed for economic dominance in Europe, often through the imperialism of acquiring colonies.

New technology made World War I different from previous wars. Allied soldiers fire at German airplanes over France in 1918. (*National Archives*)

The stalemate of trench warfare led to extremely high fatalities in World War I. These German soldiers wear masks to protect themselves from gas attacks. *(National Archives)*

Each side also took advantage of technological advances to compete in a tremendous military buildup. Technology had produced battleships and machine guns, railroads that could carry armies great distances, and airplanes that could observe enemy locations. The most frightening technology of all was probably the development of chemical weapons. To be prepared for war, each side used conscription, the forcing of male citizens to join the military forces, to create huge standing armies.

Along with the colonial expansion of European powers came strong feelings of nationalism, the belief that people who shared the same ethnic origin, language, and political ideas were entitled to independence. There were many small kingdoms within Europe that were under foreign control. European boundaries were causing conflict.

France and Germany nearly went to war in 1906 and 1911 over colonial interests in Morocco, but the center of the storm was the Balkan peninsula in southern Europe. The area consisted of two Slavic countries, Bulgaria and Serbia, and two non-Slavic countries, Greece and Romania. The countries had had many disputes with each other over the years over boundaries and cultural differences. To make matters worse, European superpowers such as Austria, Russia, and the Ottoman Empire (now Turkey) had intervened in the disputes for their own interests.

Two Balkan wars in 1912 and 1913 resolved little and set the stage for the incident that would ignite World War I. The wars left a Serbian province, Bosnia, under the rule of the Austro-Hungarian Empire, and in Serbia, a strong nationalist movement demanded freedom for Bosnia. On June 28, 1914, the Archduke Franz Ferdinand, heir to the throne of the Austro-Hungarian

Empire, and his wife Sophie were assassinated in Sarajevo, the capital of Bosnia. The assassin was Gavrilo Princip, a Serbian nationalist who wanted Bosnia returned to Serbia.

Several weeks of peace negotiations proved futile, and on July 28, 1914, Austria declared war on Serbia. The commitments of the alliances led to many other declarations of war and on August 4, 1914, Germany sent troops into Belgium to invade France. World War I, the deadliest conflict the world had ever seen, had begun. At first, it was the Central Powers—Germany and Austria-Hungary—against the Allies—France, Belgium, Great Britain, and Russia. (Italy withdrew from the Triple Alliance and eventually sided with the Allies.) As the war progressed, the Ottoman Empire and Bulgaria joined the Central Powers while 24 nations around the world joined the Allies.

TRENCH WARFARE

World War I was fought on several fronts. On the Eastern front, Germany was able to drive Russian troops back into Russia and cause so many losses that Russia was not

African-American soldiers dig trenches—not for warfare but for burial of dead soldiers at Fère-en-Tardenois, France, in 1918. *(Library of Congress)*

THE WAR AROUND THE WORLD

As its name indicates, World War I was not just fought in the trenches of Europe. Two other key battle areas were the Middle East, where the British forces led the fight against the Ottomans and German colonies in Africa. (The Ottoman Empire stretched across the Middle East, and the Ottomans ruled from their base of power in what is now Turkey.) The Middle East battleground was a stalemate until 1917 when British troops captured the key cities of Gaza (Egypt), Jerusalem (Israel), and Baghdad (Iraq). By October 1918, Ottoman forces were in retreat throughout the Middle East. The British captured Lebanon and Syria, and the Ottomans asked for an armistice.

The Middle East campaign saw the brilliant leadership of one of the war's heroes, British Colonel T. E. Lawrence, also known as Lawrence of Arabia. Lawrence led an Arab revolt against the Ottomans, successfully capturing the key port of Al Aqaba and crippling the Ottoman railway. The following year, Lawrence and his Arab soldiers helped the British take Lebanon and Syria, ending Ottoman rule in the Middle East.

German colonies in Africa at the start of the war included Togoland, the Cameroons, German Southwest Africa, and German East Africa. All fell early in the war to Allied forces except for German East Africa, where fighting continued throughout the war. German troops were launching a major offensive against the Allies when the European armistice was declared. Fighting continued for three more days before the German commander surrendered.

In June 1917, W. E. B. DuBois led 15,000 people in a silent march down Fifth Avenue in New York protesting racial violence in the United States.

a factor in the war after 1915. On the Serbian front, Central Power troops conquered Serbia by the end of 1915. However, these victories were not decisive. The outcome of the war would depend on who won the Western front, where a horrible stalemate developed.

Germany was able to advance its troops into Belgium and northeastern France, but a strong defense by France at the Battle of the Marne stopped the advance. By the end of 1914, each side had set up a line of trenches that extended more than 450 miles from Switzerland to the English Channel. The lines were just a few hundred feet apart and the land in between was known as no man's land. For the next four years, each side tried to advance and break the other's line with little if any success. It came to be known as trench warfare and resulted in tremendously high casualties. In one battle at Champagne, France, in September 1914, there were 242,000 allied deaths and 141,000 German deaths.

Two other aspects of trench warfare added to its horror. Because an attack could come at any time, soldiers had to live in the trenches, which became infested with disease-spreading rats and insects. Contagious

diseases such as cholera became epidemic among the troops and took nearly as many lives as combat. World War I also saw the introduction of chemical warfare. It was first used in 1915 when German troops released cylinders of chlorine gas on French troops, causing vomiting and suffocation. Before the war was over, other chemicals such as mustard gas would be used by both the Central Powers and the Allies.

On the day the *Lusitania* left New York, there were warnings in morning newspapers for Americans not to sail on British ships. *(New York Times)*

WILSON AND U.S. NEUTRALITY

The first reaction of most Americans to the war was a strong desire to stay out of it. President Wilson immediately declared U.S. neutrality, saying, "We must be neutral in fact as well as name, in thought as well as in action," but he knew it would be difficult. The U.S. population included millions of immigrants from the European nations involved, and their feelings were not neutral. Thousands of immigrants returned to their homelands to join the fight. Some Americans joined them. For instance, the Lafayette Escadrille, part of the French air force, consisted of American volunteers.

After the sinking of the *Lusitania* in 1915, President Wilson found it increasingly hard to keep America neutral. *(New York Times)*

The debate within the country became heated. Pacifist groups such as Jane Addams's Women's Peace Party strongly opposed any U.S. military intervention. Newspapers at the time, especially the yellow press, generally urged that the United States enter the war on the Allied side. A growing group of Americans, led by Teddy Roosevelt, called for the United States to at least be prepared for war by increasing arms and training more soldiers.

The United States maintained a military neutrality for the first part of the war, but not an economic one. In the first two years of the war, trade with the Central Powers declined from $169 million to $1 million while trade with the Allies increased from $825 million to $3 billion. U.S. loans to the Allies during the same time totaled $2.3 billion with only $27 million going to the Central Powers.

The huge war business created a booming economy for the United States, but Germany protested strongly because it meant the Allies could buy weapons, food, and other war supplies while Germany could not. Germany's lack of trade and its weakened economy also meant starvation within Germany was reaching critical levels. Germany responded by using its U-boats, or submarines, to sink all commercial ships, including U.S. ones, bound for Allied ports.

On May 7, 1915, a German U-boat sank the British passenger ship the *Lusitania* off the coast of Ireland, killing 1,198 people, including 128 Americans. The ship was carrying armaments for Great Britain, but all the dead were civilians. It was the first in a series of events that would force Wilson's involvement and strain U.S. neutrality.

Many in the United States used the sinking of the *Lusitania* as a battle cry to enter the war, but Wilson resisted. Instead, he demanded that Germany stop unrestricted submarine attacks and issue warnings to commercial ships so that innocent passengers could escape. This had been the common naval warfare practice up to that time. German leaders refused to make any concessions directly to Wilson, but they did give secret orders to the U-boat commanders not to attack passenger ships.

The crisis died down until August 1915 when a German U-boat sunk a passenger ship named the *Arabic.* Wilson was desperate to keep the United States out of the war. He said, "There is such a thing as a nation being so right that it does not need to convince others by force that it is right." He again simply demanded that Germany stop unrestricted attacks. Germany responded by telling Wilson that its U-boat commanders had been given orders not to attack passenger ships without warning.

In March, 1916, German U-boats sunk a British steamer, the *Sussex.* Wilson issued an ultimatum to Germany that it publicly declare a policy that unrestricted attacks would stop. If Germany refused, Wilson would sever diplomatic ties, the first step to declaring war. Germany knew that the U.S. entry into the war would mean defeat for the Central Powers, so they agreed to Wilson's demand. They issued the Sussex Pledge to stop unrestricted naval attacks.

"By 1917, the glory had passed from war. Young men saw soldiering as cruel duty rather than as sport."

—Secretary of War Newton D. Baker on the necessity of a draft for World War I

"War is no longer Samson with his shield and spear and David with his sling. It is the conflict of smokestacks now, the combat of the driving wheel and the engine."

—Secretary of War Newton D. Baker on preparing the United States for World War I

Propaganda posters appeared throughout America encouraging support for the war.
(Library of Congress)

The arrival of American troops in 1918, like the decorated aviator above, turned the tide in the war toward the Allies.
(Smithsonian Institute)

Wilson was narrowly reelected in November 1916, defeating Republican Charles Evans Hughes. His campaign slogan was, "He kept us out of war," but Wilson knew war was closer than ever. He started his second term trying to negotiate what he called a "peace without victory" agreement between the two sides without success. Germany's situation was especially desperate. The war front was a hopeless stalemate and at home, the German people were starving to death with some estimates as high as 1 million deaths. Germany gambled that America would not enter the war and renounced the Sussex Pledge in January 1917.

On February 3, 1917, a German U-boat sank an American ship, the *Housatonic,* and Wilson severed diplomatic ties with Germany. On March 1, the United States was given an intercepted letter from German foreign minister Arthur Zimmermann to the German ambassador in Mexico directing him what to do if the United States entered the war. In the letter, Germany promised to help Mexico win back territory lost to the United States if Mexico entered the war against the Allies. On March 16, German U-boats sank three U.S. ships, the *City of Memphis,* the *Illinois,* and the *Vigilancia.* Wilson felt he had no choice but to ask Congress to declare war. In his message to them on April 2, he said, "The world must be made safe for democracy." Congress overwhelmingly voted to approve the declaration.

THE UNITED STATES ENTERS THE WAR

President Wilson knew that preparing for the war meant much more than sending troops and supplies to Europe. The battlefields were not on American soil, but Wilson knew many of the war's effects would be felt at home. He said he feared the American people would "forget there ever was such a thing as tolerance. To fight you must be brutal and ruthless, and the spirit of ruthless brutality will enter into the very fiber of our national life,

infecting Congress, courts, the policeman on the beat, the man in the street."

When the United States declared war on Germany in April, 1917, it had fewer than 200,000 poorly trained soldiers in its military. Wilson knew it would take at least 1 to 2 million troops to win the war. He authorized the first draft since the Civil War. On June 5, 1917, ten million American men registered with the new Selective Service System. On July 20 and 21, the first group of 687,000 draftees were chosen and told to report for military training and active duty.

Wilson said, "It's not an army we must train, it is a nation." The American people had to unite behind the war for the military effort to succeed. Wilson formed the Committee on Public Information (CPI) and put George Creel, a progressive journalist, in charge of it. Creel called the efforts of the CPI "advertising," but it was really propaganda, one-sided information designed simply

Soldiers trained for the hand-to-hand combat that took place in the no-man's-land between the opposing trenches. *(Army News Features)*

"I can predict with absolute certainty that within another generation, there will be another world war if the nations of the world do not concert the method by which to prevent it."

—President Wilson in urging the formation of the League of Nations

NONCOMBAT SOLDIERS: AMERICAN WOMEN AT WAR

Two million American men were sent overseas during World War I, and their efforts helped win the war for the Allies. There were thousands more Americans whose work was just as important and often overlooked. U.S. women joined the war effort both in the military and on the home front.

Women in the military were not allowed in combat, but they served in many other ways. The first group called to duty was the Army Nurse Corps, who tended to the wounded and sick soldiers. Many served in the Women's Army Motor Corps, delivering supplies and transporting doctors and patients. Women in the Army Signal Corps were called Hello Girls because most spoke French and they were the telephone operators on the military phones. In the Navy, female yeomen handled clerical duties.

On the home front, Wilson's CPI told women it was their patriotic duty to work, and one million took on jobs outside the home during the war. Many worked at jobs directly related to the war effort, in shipyards and ammunition factories, while others took office jobs left behind by departing servicemen. When the war was over, however, most women lost their new jobs as the wartime industries slowed down and soldiers returned home and needed work.

With American men on the battlefields in Europe, many women found work in factories producing war-related goods. (*Library of Congress*)

to convince Americans that the war was right.

To secure U.S. support and loyalty, the CPI sent daily news releases to newspapers and organized 75,000 speakers to tour the country and give patriotic speeches. It also distributed millions of pamphlets and posters whose main message was that American soldiers were heroes fighting for freedom and enemy soldiers were sub-humans fighting for barbarism. Many of the pamphlets were in German, Italian, and Russian to try to convince immigrants of the war's justness.

The other half of the propaganda war was the suppression of the First Amendment right to free speech. Wilson passed the Espionage Act in 1917 and the Sedition Act in 1918 to further encourage loyalty at home. The Espionage Act made it a crime to aid the enemy and it gave the postmaster general the authority to ban any mail viewed as treasonous. The Sedition Act went even further. It made it a crime to speak, write, or publish any material opposing the war or the government.

There were still groups in the country who opposed the war, including Socialists, pacifists, and the radical union known as the Industrial Workers of the World (IWW). Both the Espionage Act and Sedition Act were enforced, which severely curtailed the efforts of these groups. The leader of American Socialism, Eugene Debs, was sentenced to ten years in prison for an anti-

Baron von Richthofen (above, right) was the most famous aviator of the war. He shot down 80 Allied planes before being shot down in 1918. *(Australian War Museum)*

"People call me an idealist. Well, that is how I know I am an American. America is the only idealistic nation in the world."

—President Wilson defending the League of Nations plan

AFRICAN-AMERICAN CONTRIBUTIONS TO THE WAR

Many African Americans saw World War I as an opportunity to show their patriotism and find their rightful place in American society. Unfortunately, it did not work out that way, although there were some temporary gains. Many job opportunities did open up for blacks, as the wartime industries desperately needed workers. Most of these jobs were in the North, which contributed to the Great Migration of blacks north during the 1910s.

Companies that had never hired African Americans before began hiring the migrants although sometimes only because of orders from the U.S. government. African Americans worked in the shipyards and ammunition factories and fared better economically and socially than they had in the South, although segregation was still a problem. When the war was over, most blacks lost their jobs to returning white soldiers reentering the job market.

The African Americans' experience in the military was not as positive. More than 370,000 blacks served in the military, but most encountered the same racism they suffered at home. Racial tension plagued black military bases during the recruits' training. In August 1917, a riot occurred in Houston, Texas, when townspeople and black soldiers clashed after some of the soldiers had been beaten. Twenty-six people died, and the military dealt harshly with the black soldiers—19 were hanged and 44 were sentenced to life imprisonment.

On the battlefield, African Americans served bravely when they were allowed to fight. Due to racism, most black troops were denied the opportunity to be in combat. One exception was Eugene Bullard, the first black fighter pilot in history. Bullard volunteered for the French Flying Corps when the war broke out and earned many French medals for his bravery. He became known as the Black Swallow of Death and after the United States entered the war, he asked to fly for the U.S. Air Corps. He was refused.

Unlike Teddy Roosevelt, President Wilson was often in ill-health while in office, suffering from recurrent headaches and stomach problems. *(Library of Congress)*

war speech. Bill Haywood, the leader of the IWW, was sentenced to 20 years for opposing the war. Before the war was over, 6,000 arrests were made based on these two laws.

Wilson also had to turn the U.S. economy into a wartime economy to produce the weapons and supplies needed by the military. First, he had the government take control of two vital industries, the railroads and shipbuilding. He then created the War Industries Board and put Wall Street broker Bernard Baruch in charge. The board had the authority to control the prices and distribution of America's raw materials. Baruch even forced car makers such as Henry Ford to stop making cars and start producing war products.

Wilson's final concern at home was raising money to pay for the war effort. Two simple steps raised $33 billion for the war. First, Wilson raised the federal income tax rates, especially on the rich. Americans with lower incomes still only paid about 4 percent, but

those with incomes over $1 million now paid 70 percent. These increased taxes raised about $10 billion, but the bulk of the money raised came from Americans buying war bonds from the government. The average American bought $400 of bonds during the war, raising about $23 billion for the government.

More than 100,000 American soldiers were killed in World War I, but survivors came home to a hero's welcome throughout the country. *(Library of Congress)*

In 1918, President Wilson became the first president to go to Europe during his term.

A great influenza epidemic spread around the world in 1918, killing 20 million people. One in four Americans contracted the disease, and 500,000 died. In some U.S. cities, people were required to wear masks to prevent the spread of the disease.

TURNING THE TIDE IN EUROPE

U.S. troops first started arriving in Europe in June 1917, but the new draftees needed considerable training. By June 1918, one million U.S. troops under the leadership of General Pershing were in Europe and playing a decisive role in battles along the Western front. The timing of the U.S. arrival was crucial.

In late 1917, a revolution in Russia overthrew the czar, or king, and a new communist government took over. The new government signed a peace treaty with Germany, which freed up one million German troops to move to the Western front. With the new troops, Germany launched an offensive that reached 37 miles outside Paris. Allied and American troops were able to stop the advance and by July 1918, German troops were retreating.

Throughout the fall of 1918, more U.S. troops arrived on the battlefields. In September more than 1 million U.S. troops took part in the Battle of Verdun, defeating the Germans. By October, 2 million American troops were in Europe, and German generals were requesting an armistice, or peace agreement, with the Allies. The Allies refused to negotiate until Germany's king, Kaiser Wilhelm II, relinquished his throne. He abdicated on November 9 and fled to Holland. The armistice ending World War I was signed on November 11.

The death tolls from the war were staggering. The Allies suffered 5.1 million deaths and the Central Powers 3.4 million. The final death toll for the U.S. was 116,000 with another 200,000 wounded. A total of 20 million soldiers were wounded, and there were an estimated 10 million civilian deaths, most of these from disease and starvation. The total cost of the war was estimated at $186 billion.

CHAPTER 7

WILSON BECOMES PEACEMAKER, 1918–1919

EVEN AFTER THE U.S. ENTERED THE WAR, President Wilson continued to work for a peace settlement. In January 1918, he presented his peace plan to Congress, a plan that became known as the Fourteen Points. His plan had three main ideas: a reduction of arms by all nations; the creation of new, independent nations within Europe by breaking up the German, Austro-Hungarian, and Ottoman empires; and the formation of an international organization to prevent future wars called the League of Nations.

Allied leaders (left to right) David Lloyd George of Britain, Georgio Soninno of Italy, Georges Clemenceau of France, and President Wilson met in Paris to settle the peace. *(National Archives)*

President Wilson was received as a hero in Europe, but his idea for a League of Nations met a bitter defeat back home in Congress. *(Library of Congress)*

"I would rather fail at a cause I knew someday will triumph than to win in a cause that I know some day will fail."

—President Wilson in arguing for the U.S. entry into the League of Nations

Wilson went to Europe after the armistice was signed and met with the Allied leaders of Great Britain, France, and Italy to propose his plan. They met at the French palace of Versailles, just outside Paris. The Allied leaders had very different ideas from Wilson, however. They insisted that Germany be punished for causing the war. The punishment included a complete disarming of Germany and a huge reparations payment of $56 billion to the Allies. Germany was also stripped of most of its colonies around the world and even 10 percent of land within its own boundaries. Nine new nations were created within Europe, but Allied nations kept their colonies, assumed control of Germany's colonies, and did not agree to arms reductions.

Wilson was very disappointed, but he did win acceptance of his most important point—the formation of the League of Nations. He reluctantly signed the peace agreement called the Treaty of Versailles on June 28, 1919, and headed home. In November 1919, his plan suffered its final defeat when the Senate refused to allow the United States to join the new League of Nations. Wilson's only consolation was winning the Nobel Peace Prize in 1919.

Wilson said that without an effective League of Nations, there would be another world war within a generation. His words could not have been more prophetic. Without a strong United States presence, the League proved ineffective, and 20 years later, world war erupted in Europe once again.

The French palace of Versailles was the home of the French kings from 1682 to 1790. After the French revolution it was owned by the French government. *(Library of Congress)*

TECHNOLOGY CHANGES THE AMERICAN HOME

Early in the 20th century, technical improvements made the transmission of electric power much cheaper and reliable. Many Americans found they could afford electricity in their home, and the effect on daily life was dramatic. There were the obvious changes of light bulbs replacing kerosene or lamps and telephones appearing in most homes, but electric power also gave rise to the household appliance.

Electric appliances that became available to Americans from 1900 to 1920 included: vacuum cleaners, toasters, irons, washing machines, record players, and hot-water heaters. American life was also made easier and more enjoyable by several non-electric gadgets such as the Brownie

Modern appliances began to make housekeeping much easier in the early 1900s. *(General Electric)*

camera, the safety razor, and the icebox. Homemakers also no longer had to can their own food to preserve it, canned food became available in their stores.

Throughout the first two decades of the century, the drudgery of homemaking was gradually being reduced. This was especially important to women, who were usually the homemakers. Women now had more time to devote to other interests. By 1920, more than 8 million women had joined the work force, many in new positions such as typists or telephone operators. Another million had joined women's clubs. Some of the clubs were simply social, but others campaigned for causes of the era such as women's suffrage and child labor.

"Make way for democracy! We saved it in France and . . . we will save it in the United States of America or know the reason why."

—W. E. B. DuBois calling for civil rights for blacks after their service to the United States in World War I

Black leader Marcus Garvey's "back to Africa" campaign emphasized black pride and economic independence. His prominence grew after World War I. *(National Archives)*

THE POSTWAR PERIOD

The final year and a half of Wilson's presidency and of the decade of the 1910s was a very difficult time for the president and the country. Just before the Senate voted down his League of Nations, Wilson suffered a serious stroke and was virtually an invalid for the remainder of his term. Partly because of his lack of leadership and partly because of national disillusionment over the war, the United States encountered severe problems on many fronts.

Labor and management united during the war to produce the supplies needed for the war effort. As soon as the war was over, however, labor problems worsened for several reasons. Inflation rose sharply during the war, and prices doubled between 1914 and 1919. This meant workers needed higher wages. Unemployment also rose as soldiers returned home looking for work, and many factory workers lost their war-related jobs.

The labor strife led to 3,000 strikes in 1919 alone, affecting 4 million workers, but this time, public support was on the side of business. Big business had helped the United States win the war, and most postwar Americans had lost their progressive ideals. Management also used lies about union leadership to gain the public's support against labor, as in the steelworkers strike.

In September 1919, 365,000 steelworkers went on strike demanding higher wages and the right to form a union. The workers still worked 12-hour days and their yearly salary was under $1,500. The company owners claimed that the strike was un-American because the workers were immigrants and their leaders were radicals or communists. Americans had a growing fear of communism since the successful communist revolution in Russia in 1917. A Senate committee upheld the company owners' claims without an investigation, and the strikers were eventually forced to go back to work with few concessions. The truth was there were no radicals in the steelworkers union movement; the workers simply wanted higher wages and recognition of their union.

PRESIDENT EDITH WILSON?

On October 2, 1919, President Wilson suffered a stroke at the White House. He had suffered strokes before, but this was a serious one. Wilson lay near death for two weeks and was incapacitated for several months. So who acted as president during that time?

Wilson's vice president Thomas Marshall would have taken over the president's duties if Wilson had died or resigned, but this was not the situation. Marshall did not know the seriousness of the president's condition because Wilson's wife, Edith, was allowing only his doctor to visit. The rest of the time, she was determining what duties were performed and how. When something needed the president's signature, she would guide his hand over the document. Edith Wilson said it was her "beloved husband I was trying to save … after that, he was the president of the United States."

It was not until April 1920 that Wilson was able to meet with his Cabinet again and the final months of his second term were uneventful. After his presidency ended, Wilson disappeared from public view and lived the rest of his life as a semi-invalid. He died in 1924. In 1967, the Twenty-fifth Amendment to the Constitution finally mandated that the vice president assume power if the president is "unable to discharge the powers and duties of his office."

In 1919, the first municipal airport in the United States opened in Tucson, Arizona.

Management continued to use Americans' fear of communists, or reds as they were called, to put down strike after strike in 1919. It led to the Red Scare of 1919–20, directed by Attorney General A. Mitchell Palmer. Palmer organized a series of raids across the country resulting in thousands of arrests and hundreds of deportations.

Minorities also became a target of general U.S. disillusion and mistrust. As a lingering effect of the war, immigrants continued to be looked upon with suspicion. They were resented for taking jobs away from the returning servicemen. Anti-immigrant feelings were also reflected in Congress passing a law in 1917 requiring all immigrants entering the United States to be literate.

It was the African Americans, however, who suffered the most in the postwar period. Despite many blacks serving bravely in the war, racism was still prevalent across the nation and growing in the north.

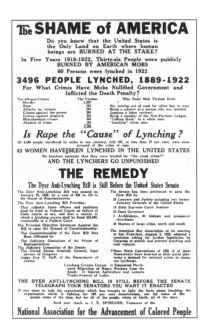

Black soldiers returned home to the same racism they had left behind. The Senate would not even pass the NAACP's anti-lynching bill. *(National Archives)*

Suffragists finally won their battle; the Nineteenth Amendment, passed in 1919, allowed women to vote. *(Library of Congress)*

By 1916, movies became the fifth largest business in America behind only railroads, textiles, iron and steel, and oil.

The great migration of blacks to northern cities between 1910 and1920 led to competition with whites for jobs and living space. Feelings of racial intolerance resulted in 28 race riots in 1919. The worst riot was in Chicago in June 1919, where 38 people died and a thousand homes were destroyed. That same year, 70 African Americans were the victims of lynchings, some while wearing their war uniforms. When the National Association for the Advancement of Colored People (NAACP) introduced an anti-lynching bill to Congress in 1919, it was killed before a vote.

The only highlight of the postwar period was Congress finally approving a measure giving women the right to vote. The Nineteenth Amendment to the constitution would be ratified a year later, and the 72-year effort for women's suffrage would finally be

WHAT CHILDREN WERE READING

As education improved and literacy rose during the early 20th century, there was much more reading material available to children. Many books started to be written particularly for children. The biggest selling book of the 1900s was Frank Baum's *The Wonderful Wizard of Oz*, published in 1900. In 1902, Rudyard Kipling's collection of *Just So Stories* encouraged kids to learn about faraway places and cultures. In 1906, Edward Stratemeyer published the first in a long line of Hardy Boys and Nancy Drew mysteries. Frances Burnett's children's classic *The Secret Garden* first appeared in 1911.

It was during this era that kids started reading the Sunday comics in huge numbers. The Sunday comics had been around since 1896, but parents objected to the excessive violence of the early comics. In 1902, Richard Outcault created the "Buster Brown" strip, and kids found it expressed their spirit of mischief perfectly, since Buster and his dog Tige were constantly in trouble. Each Buster Brown strip ended with a moral of what Buster had learned, making parents happy too. Similar strips such as "Mutt and Jeff" and "The Katzenjammer Kids" appeared and consumer parents had another reason to buy the Sunday newspaper.

Another very popular format was that of the dime-store novels. The stories were more like long short stories published in magazine form and sold for five or ten cents. The magazines had such names as *Brave and Bold, Pluck and Luck,* and *Might and Main* and featured the adventures of young heroes. The heroes always exhibited the qualities of the ideal American boy at the time — moral, athletic, brave, and ambitious. The most famous character of them all was Frank Merriwell, written for 20 years by George Patten, alias Burt L. Standish. As a Yale College student, Merriwell excelled at all sports and could even make a baseball curve in two directions. After college he fought Chinese bandits, Texas outlaws, and big city criminals, while loving his mother and his country and disapproving of alcohol. The stories' combination of adventure and social conscience had great appeal to the youth of the era.

EDISON FILMS TO BE RELEASED FROM MAY 11 TO 18 INCLUSIVE

Thomas Edison invented the first motion-picture machine, the kinetoscope, in 1893. Edison's company would dominate the early years of American movies.
(Private Collection)

victorious. Also in 1919, a disastrous constitutional amendment, Prohibition, went into effect prohibiting the production, distribution, sale, and consumption of alcohol. The law would prove unpopular and lead to the establishment of huge crime organizations over the next 14 years before it would be repealed.

In 1920, suffragist Carrie Chapman Catt started the League of Women Voters to educate the millions of new female voters. The League still exists today, organizing debates and distributing voter information.

Americans had more leisure time, and technology helped them enjoy it. Radio brought news, soap operas, and sports, especially baseball, into the home, and eager youngsters constructed their own kit radios to hear the broadcasts.
(Carnegie Library)

> *"If I'm going to be embarrassed in public, I'll have to have more money."*
>
> —Mary Pickford asking D. W. Griffith for a raise

One of the biggest movie stars of the 1910s was Mary Pickford. She was also known as America's Sweetheart because of her popularity.
(Private Collection)

LEISURE TIME

The lifestyle of Americans changed considerably throughout the first two decades of the 20th century. Much of this was due to the changing economy. First, industry and mass production meant there were more products for Americans and they were cheaper. Americans were becoming consumers and as their wages increased, a new middle class was forming. Working hours were also decreasing so this new middle class had more leisure time to enjoy things like the movies and baseball.

Movies

Thomas Edison had invented the basic technology of the movies in the 1880s and by the 1890s, his company was producing short films. Edison's films were more a novelty than anything else; they were usually under one minute long and showed simple scenes, such as a man sneezing or waves crashing on a shore.

TRAVELING SHOWS

At the turn of the century, small towns in America were still quite isolated, particularly in terms of available entertainment. As a result, entertainment came to the towns and traveling shows flourished. The most popular of these were circuses, vaudeville, and chautauquas and the arrival of one of these shows might be the only entertainment a town would have all year.

Circuses were at their height in 1906 when 109 troupes were touring the country. The two biggest were Ringling Brothers and Barnum and Bailey's and each tried to be the greatest show on Earth, as their advertising put it. Circuses would try to drum up business by first staging a parade through town showing off their brightly colored wagons, wild animals, and calliopes, or pipe organs. The larger circuses featured so many performers, they needed three rings to exhibit them all, and families would marvel at the clowns, trapeze artists, and lion tamers.

Almost every town in America had a theater where vaudevillians could come and perform. The vaudeville troupe included some of the biggest stars of the day including singers, dancers and comedians. It would also feature lesser known novelty acts such as jugglers, magicians, and animal acts. Vaudeville remained America's favorite form of entertainment until the 1930s when the movies took away most of its biggest stars. Vaudevillians such as Buster Keaton, Charlie Chaplin, and W.C. Fields would eventually leave the vaudeville stage for the better pay of Hollywood.

The chautauqua was a uniquely American form of entertainment. Teddy Roosevelt called it " the most American thing in America." Named after a summer festival held yearly on Lake Chautauqua in New York, this traveling show featured light entertainment, including brass bands and singers. The show also tried to be educational by including opera divas, poetry readings, or an excerpt from a Shakespeare play. The show would usually end with motivational speeches on reform, religion, or positive thinking. At its height, 40 million Americans attended chauatauqua shows every summer. As radio grew in popularity in the 1920s and 1930s, the chautauqua would fade away.

In 1903, *The Great Train Robbery* was released. This 12-minute film told a story and the U.S. public wanted more. Movie theaters (called nickelodeons because admission cost a nickel) started opening across the country. By 1910, there were 10,000 nickelodeons, and movie attendance was about 26 million a week.

Charlie Chaplin's silent comedies where he played a character known simply as The Tramp were immensely popular.
(Private Collection)

Pictured in the front row from left to right: D. W. Griffith, Mary Pickford, Charlie Chaplin, and Douglas Fairbanks, formed United Artists Corporation in 1919 to control their own movie distribution. Two studio executives look on. (*Private Collection*)

"*Europe was devastated by the war, we by the aftermath.*"

—Supreme Court Justice Louis Brandeis on the postwar period in the United States

As movies became a big business, the industry suffered from a common problem of the era—a trust formed. Edison had joined forces with several other companies, including Eastman Kodak who made the film, to eliminate competition. New independent film companies found a way to avoid the trust's control and make their own movies—they moved to California. In an area outside Los Angeles called Hollywood, they found wide-open spaces, year-round good weather, and freedom from the control of the trust. By 1914, there were 52 companies in the area buying up huge tracts of land.

Several developments made the 1910s film's most important decade. As the new Hollywood companies competed for viewers, films became longer and the stories more dramatic. Directors started using techniques such as the closeup, fadeout, and flashback to make their stories more interesting to watch. In 1915, director D. W. Griffith made the three-hour long epic *Birth of a Nation*. The film has been condemned for its glorification of the KKK and racist attitude toward blacks, but its technical innovations in storytelling set the stage for decades of Hollywood films.

In the 1910s, the star system was also born, as movie fans wanted to know who their favorite actors and actresses were. Westerns were very popular at the time, and Tom Mix and William S. Hart were big Western stars. Douglas Fairbanks was very popular in adventure films. The biggest stars of the decade, however, were the romantic heroine Mary Pickford and the slapstick comedian Charlie Chaplin. As these stars' fame rose, so did their salaries. By the end of the decade, each was making $1 million a year.

Another development that modernized the film industry was the building of new theaters often called movie palaces. Most nickelodeons were little more than storefronts with small screens and uncomfortable folding chairs. The new movie houses built during the 1910s were spacious and tried to create an atmosphere of luxury. They could seat hundreds comfortably, and screens were much larger. Decor was often lavish, highlighted by huge chandeliers hanging from high ceilings.

By the end of the decade, more than 25 million Americans were going to the movies every day, a remarkable number in a country with a total population of about 100 million. All the key elements of today's movies but one, sound, were established during the 1910s. Sound would come in 1927.

Baseball

By the turn of the century, baseball had already become America's national pastime. It had been popular since the Civil War, when soldiers would play the game in their camps. Organized leagues and professional players had been around since the 1880s, and fans had their first heroes in players such as Cap Anson, Napoleon Lajoie, and King Kelly.

The word *movies* was originally used by Hollywood locals to describe all the people involved in making films. It later came to mean the films themselves.

"The invention of the photoplay [movies] is as great a step as was the beginning of picture writing in the Stone Age."

—American poet Vachel Lindsay on the importance of movies

A three-man Baseball Commission (man on right is a secretary) governed baseball from 1903 until 1920. Ban Johnson (second from right) was the innovator of the World Series. *(National Baseball Hall of Fame and Library)*

Christy Mathewson was a star pitcher for the New York Giants from 1900 to 1916. In the 1905 World Series, he won three games, all shut-outs. *(Bucknell University)*

In 1900, the American League (AL) joined the National League (NL) as the two major baseball leagues and for three years, the leagues tried to outbid each other for the best players. The owners quickly realized this bidding war was bad for their profits, so they reached an agreement in 1903. The agreement basically gave owners the ability to control players' salaries by binding them by contract to one team for their entire career unless the owners traded them. This standard part of every player's contract was called the reserve clause, and it would make baseball players powerless as employees for decades.

Attendance grew steadily from 4 million in 1900 to 7 million in 1910 and over 9 million in 1919. As attendance grew, most cities built new, bigger stadiums, including the Polo Grounds in New York, which could seat more than 32,000 fans. Attendance was particularly high during the World Series at the end of the year, which pitted the AL champion against the NL champion. The first World Series was held in 1903, and the AL's Boston Beaneaters beat the Pittsburgh Pirates five games to three. (The next year, the Beaneaters became the Red Sox.)

Those fans who could not attend followed their teams in the newspapers, which now had writers assigned to cover the team. Such writers as Ring Lardner and Damon Runyon gave colorful accounts of the era's best players. These included Ty Cobb, the game's best hitter with a record .367 lifetime batting average, and Walter Johnson, the era's best pitcher with 413 lifetime wins.

The Boston Red Sox would dominate the first two decades of the century winning five World Series, but the star system also existed in baseball. Fans of losing teams were often just as interested in following the feats of their favorite players, some of whom were both great players and fascinating personalities. The New York Giants had pitcher Christy Mathewson, the All-American boy who never recovered from his World War I injuries. Pittsburgh had shortstop Honus Wagner, who refused to let a cigarette company issue his baseball card because he disapproved of smoking. The Chicago Cubs had pitcher Mordechai Brown, whose pitching hand only had three fingers due to a childhood

Ty Cobb (driving the car on the right) ended the 1910 season in a tie with Nap Lajoie for highest batting average, and both men were awarded cars by automaker Hugh Chalmers. *(National Baseball Hall of Fame and Library)*

"Shoeless Joe" Jackson (seen batting) was one of the stars of baseball before he took part in the "fixed" 1919 World Series. *(AP/Wide World Photos)*

accident. The Philadelphia A's had Frank "Home Run" Baker who hit homers in an era when they were rare. The Chicago White Sox had "Shoeless Joe" Jackson, the game's second best hitter who ran so fast, he ran out of his shoes.

The game was at its height of popularity when a terrible scandal that nearly destroyed it was uncovered. "Shoeless Joe" and the Chicago White Sox were at the center of it all. In 1919, professional gambler Arnold Rothstein offered White Sox first baseman Chick Gandil $100,000 to fix the World Series so that the White Sox would lose to the Cincinnati Reds. Gandil got several of his teammates, including Jackson, to agree to throw, or intentionally lose, the Series, and the White Sox lost to the Reds five games to three.

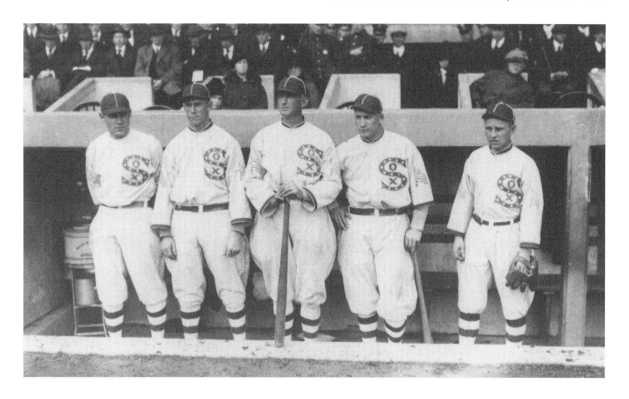

Eight players were eventually implicated in the fix. Jackson apparently just accepted some of the bribe money but did not intentionally lose, because he was the batting star of the Series, hitting .375 and the only home run. Another player, Buck Weaver, just knew of the plot and did not report it. The Black Sox, as they came to be known, were acquitted in court when their confessions mysteriously disappeared, but the new commissioner of baseball, Kenesaw Mountain Landis, barred them from the game for life.

It is uncertain if Landis's move alone would have restored the game's integrity, but baseball had another rising star who would make it more popular than ever. In 1919, Babe Ruth hit 29 home runs for the Boston Red Sox, shattering the previous home-run record. It was just the beginning. The next year, the Red Sox sold Ruth to the New York Yankees and Ruth would spend the next 15 years not just saving the game, but becoming its all-time legendary hero.

Joe Jackson leans on a bat, standing with the 1918 White Sox outfielders. *(National Baseball Hall of Fame and Library)*

"Say it ain't so, Joe."

—A young boy outside the Black Sox trial for throwing the 1919 World Series pleading with "Shoeless Joe" Jackson

GLOSSARY

anarchism The theory that all types of government are inherently evil and should be destroyed.

armistice The ending of a war by mutual consent.

assembly line A line of factory workers and equipment where a product is assembled as it passes from worker to worker.

blues A style of music that evolved from several different African-American styles with slow tempos and sad lyrics.

chemical warfare Warfare using poisons and gases as weapons.

communism A system of government in which the state controls all means of production and establishes a social order where all goods are shared equally.

conscription The forcing of citizens to join the military forces.

dyslexia A learning disability affecting the ability to read.

espionage The use of spies to obtain secret information.

homesteaders Settlers of land offered by the government who promise in return to work and improve the land.

imperialism A policy of extending a country's authority by acquisition of land or economic or political influence.

Industrial Revolution The widespread replacement of manual labor by machines that began in Britain in the 18th century and spread to America in the 19th century, which resulted in great social and economic changes.

isolationism A policy of avoiding economic or political involvement with other countries.

jazz A style of music evolved from African-American styles such as ragtime and blues that emphasizes a strong beat, regular rhythm, and improvisation.

laissez faire A government policy not to interfere in the affairs of business.

locks Dams with gates that open and close to raise or lower water levels and ships to different levels.

lynching To hang a person without due process of law.

martial law Temporary rule by the military when civil authority breaks down.

muckrakers Writers who exposed society's problems.

nationalism   A belief that a people who share the same ethnic origin, language, and political ideas deserve political independence.

nickelodeon   An early movie house charging a nickel admission.

pacifism   The belief that disputes between nations should be settled without the use of war.

progressive movement   A movement composed of reformers seeking changes in societal problems such as poverty, child labor, unfair business practices, and workers and women's rights.

Prohibition   A law banning the production, distribution, sale, and consumption of alcohol.

propaganda   One-sided information designed to promote a political cause.

ragtime   A style of music evolved from African-American styles marked by an emphasis on melody and beat.

reparations Compensation that a defeated nation is required to pay as punishment after a war.

robber baron   A 19th-century businessman who became wealthy by unethical means.

sedition   Behavior or language that encourages others to rebel against the authority of the government.

segregation   The policy of imposing the separation of groups by race and other social differences.

socialism   A system of government where the production of goods is owned and regulated by the community as a whole.

standpatters   Conservatives who believe in little or no political or social change.

sweatshop   A factory where people work under unsafe conditions for low wages.

tariff   A tax imposed by the government on imported and exported goods.

tenements   Poor, run-down buildings, often in slums.

trust   A combination of businesses intended to eliminate competition.

U-boats   German submarines.

union   An alliance of workers intended to strengthen their demands for rights such as fair pay, safe working conditions, etc.

yellow journalism   Journalism that distorts or sensationalizes the news to attract readers and promote a point of view.

FURTHER READING

Angel, Ann. *America in the 20th Century: 1900–1909.* Tarrytown, N.Y.: Marshall Cavendish, 1995.

———. *America in the 20th Century: 1910–1919.* Tarrytown, N.Y.: Marshall Cavendish, 1995

Batchelor, Bob. *The 1900s.* Westport, Conn.: Greenwood Press, 2002.

Blanke, David. *The 1910s.* Westport, Conn.: Greenwood Press, 2002.

Burgan, Michaelo. *William Howard Taft.* Mankato, Minn.: Compass Point, 2003.

Carlson, Peter. *Roughneck: The Life and Times of Big Bill Haywood.* New York: Norton, 1983.

Coffey, Michael, ed. With Terry Golway. *The Irish in America.* Boston: Hyperion, 1997.

Cohen, Michael P. *The Pathless Way: John Muir and the American Wilderness.* Madison: University of Wisconsin Press, 1984.

Cooper, John Milton, Jr. *The Warrior and the Priest: Woodrow Wilson and Theodore Roosevelt.* Cambridge, Mass.: Belknap, 1985.

Craats, Rennay. *America Through the Decades: The 1900s.* Mankato, Minn.: Weigl, 2001.

———. *America Through the Decades: The 1910s.* Mankato, Minn.: Weigl, 2001.

Devlin, Patrick. *Too Proud to Fight: Woodrow Wilson's Neutrality.* New York: Oxford, 1985.

Di Franco, J. Philip. *The Italian-American Experience.* New York: Doherty, 1988.

Dolan, Edward F. *The Spanish-American War.* Brookfield, Conn.: Millbrook, 2001.

Durrett, Deanne. *The 1900s.* Farmington Hills, Mich.: Greenhaven, 2004.

———. *The 1910s.* Farmington Hills, Mich.: Greenhaven, 2004.

Eisenhower, John S. D. *Intervention: The United States Involvement in the Mexican Revolution.* New York: Norton, 1995.

Evans, Harold. *The American Century.* New York: Knopf, 2000.

Feinstein, Stephen. *The 1900s: From Teddy Roosevelt to Flying Machines.* Berkeley Heights, N.J.: Enslow, 2001.

———. *The 1910s: From World War I to Ragtime Music.* Berkeley Heights, N.J.: Enslow, 2001.

Golay, Michael. *Spanish-American War.* New York: Facts On File, 2003.

Gould, Lewis L. *The Presidency of Theodore Roosevelt.* Lawrence: University of Kansas Press, 1991.

Green, Robert. *Theodore Roosevelt.* Mankato, Minn.: Compass Point, 2003.

———. *Woodrow Wilson.* Mankato, Minn.: Compass Point, 2003.

Greenwood, Janette Thomas. *The Gilded Age: A History in Documents.* New York: Oxford, 2000.

Hakim, Joy. *An Age of Extremes: 1870–1917.* New York: Oxford University Press, 1999.

Hobsbawm, E. J. *The Age of Empire, 1875–1914.* New York: Vintage, 1989.

Hofstadter, Richard. *The Age of Reform.* New York: Knopf, 1989.

Immel, Myra H., ed. *The 1900s.* Farmington Hills, Mich.: Greenhaven, 2000.

James, Lawrence. *The Golden Warrior: The Life and Legend of T. E. Lawrence.* London: Weidenfeld and Nicolson, 1994.

Jeffers, H. Paul. *Colonel Roosevelt: Theodore Roosevelt Goes to War, 1897–1898.* New York: Wiley, 1996.

Jennings, Peter, and Todd Brewster. *The Century for Young People*. New York: Doubleday, 1999.

Johnson, J. H. *Stalemate! Great Trench Warfare Battles of 1915–1917*. New York: Arms and Armor/Sterling, 1995.

Katz, William Loren. *A History of Multicultural America: The Great Migrations, 1880s–1912*. Austin, Tex.: RSVP, 1998

———. *A History of Multicultural America: The New Freedom to the New Deal, 1913–1939*. Austin, Tex.: RSVP, 1996.

Keegan, John. *An Illustrated History of the First World War*. New York: Knopf, 2001.

Kendall, Martha. *Failure Is Impossible! The History of American Women's Rights*. Minneapolis, Minn.: 2001.

Kent, Noel Jacob. *America in 1900*. Armonk, N.Y.: M.E. Sharpe, 2000

Lesy, Michael. *Dreamland: America at the Dawn of the Twentieth Century*. New York: New Press, 1997.

Levinson, Nancy Smiler. *Turn of the Century*. New York: Lodestar, 1994.

McCullough, David. *The Path Between the Seas: The Creation of the Panama Canal, 1870–1914*. New York: Simon and Schuster, 1978.

Mee, Charles. *The End of Order: Versailles, 1919*. New York: Dutton, 1983.

Miller, James. *The 1900s*. Farmington Hills, Mich.: Greenhaven, 2001.

Milton, Joyce. *The Yellow Kids: Foreign Correspondents in the Heyday of Yellow Journalism*. New York: Harper & Row, 1989.

Musicant, Ivan. *Empire by Default*. New York: Henry Holt, 1998.

Reckner, James R. *Teddy Roosevelt's Great White Fleet*. Annapolis, Md.: Naval Institute Press, 1988.

Rose, Cynthia, ed. *1900–1919*. Farmington Hills, Mich., Gale, 2002.

Rubel, David. *The United States in the 20th Century*. New York: Scholastic, 1995.

Samuels, Peggy, and Harold Samuels. *Remembering the Maine*. Washington, D.C.: Smithsonian, 1995.

Sweeney, William. *History of the American Negro in the Great World War*. Westwood, Conn.: Greenwood, 1974.

Time-Life Editors. *Dawn of the Century: 1900–1910*. Alexandria, Va.: Time-Life Books, 1998.

———. *End of Innocence: 1910–1920*. Alexandria, Va.: Time-Life Books, 1998.

Tompkins, Vincent. *American Decades: 1900–1909*. Farmington Hills, Mich.: Gale, 1996.

———. *American Decades: 1910–1919*. Farmington Hills, Mich.: Gale, 1996.

Traxel, David. *1898: The Birth of the American Century*. New York: Knopf, 1998.

Uschan, Michael V. *The 1910s*. Farmington Hills, Mich.: Lucent Books, 1999.

Woog, Adam. *The 1900s*. Farmington Hills, Mich.: Lucent Books, 1999.

Wukovits, John F. *The 1910s*. Farmington Hills, Mich.: Greenhaven, 2000.

Yapp, Nicholas, and Konemann, Inc., eds. *Decades of the 20th Century: The 1900s*. New York: Konemann, 2003.

———. *Decades of the 20th Century: The 1910s*. New York: Konemann, 2003.

INDEX